True Buddhism

Quantum Life Buddhism Study Materials

Sifu Sylvain Chamberlain-Nyudo

More information on Quantum Life
Buddhism at:

http://threefoldlotus.com

&

http://www.lulu.com/kwoon

Distributed in the United States and Canada by: the Threefold Lotus Kwoon as the Threefold Lotus Kwoon Press in partnership with LULU.com

ISBN: 978-0-557-25856-7

First Edition

Printed in the United States of America

More from the Threefold Lotus Kwoon

There is no I

Nagarjuna

Kumarajiva

Vasubandhu

Some Sutras

Study for the Lotus Sutra

Mahaparinirvana Sutra

Ongi Kuden

The Science of Mind

Beyond Zen

Question the Corridors

The Way

Threefold Lotus Kwoon Student Manual

TLK Instruction Workbook

Meditation for Enlightenment

Meditation for Health and Vitality

The Mental Edge

Quantum Life Buddhist Liturgy - Gongyo

Table of Contents

Introduction

Buddhism has become a global practice. Buddhism is not a "religion" as we think of religion in the West. Even so, there are so many branches and sects of "Buddhism" that people, especially in the West, but also in much of the East are completely misled or misinformed as to the essential and true teachings of the Buddha.

There are a plethora of books and papers written on the subject of Buddhism from scholarly to fiction, which attempt to define Buddhism, in part, in total, or in minute sub sects or periods of history. It is not the goal of this writing to disprove, argue, validate, or even to surmise the efforts of these many writings.

What I will attempt here is the grand overview as much as the insistence and constant striving to return always to the Buddha's actual teachings. As Buddhism traveled all over India, to Sri Lanka, Malaysia, Thailand, Viet Nam, then to China's South, and then into Tibet and China's North and to Korea, Japan and all of Asia over hundreds of years, it might be expected that teachings would gather local culture, legend, gods, and regional parables. Both the time of travel and the destinations of travel have accounted for endless regional developments of the Buddhas actual teachings. Even the fact that the Buddha's teachings span some fifty years or more lends to this situation. However, as many notable scholars have done over the thousands of years since the Buddha's spoken words, men who dedicated their entire lives to the correct transmission of the Buddha's teachings, I will do my best to walk right past those esoteric and extraneous bits of lore and focus solely on the teachings as taught by the Buddha's words and these few notable scholars, to provide you, the reader, as accurate and concise a framework of the true teachings, the essential and core teachings of the Buddha. In contrast to Western and most of all other world teachings of the era, the Buddha taught verbally, and his teachings were repeated verbatim. These teachings were repeated over and over, to be memorized, in order to be both learned and transmitted or taught to others. This was the order of the day. As the Buddha's passing became imminent, the head monks where the Buddha's teachings were daily repeated, began to inscribe the teachings from the verbal repetitions in a specialized script of Sanskrit in order to more tightly control the exact language of the teachings as uttered by the Buddha himself. This means that there exist a tremendous amount of written texts transcribed directly from the Buddha's very words.

The Buddha's teachings are not complicated, but they are extremely profound. The Buddha's teachings are statements that are elucidated with scientific rigor, and proved out through demonstration, testing through practice, and actual results.

Buddhism is a Life Science. Devoid of mysticism and lore, Buddhism is focused observation on the nature of life, suffering, and the elimination of suffering for all sentient creatures.

For millennia, Doctors, Psychologists, Philosophers, Engineers, Architects, Poets, Scientists, and many others, have been trying to find fountains of youth, cure-alls, pills, treatments, "perfection" of all types to provide humankind with indestructible happiness and security. Buddhism teaches us how we, by ourselves, can achieve the goal of indestructible happiness and security in our present form and in this lifetime through daily practice and training of the way we perceive and think of life and the world around us.

Special Thanks

I owe a gratitude to Sandra Lee Hendrix for her tireless readings and re-readings of drafts of this manuscript and her willingness to discuss passages and references that I too often make that require better definition and clarity. She is a true ally and supporter.

Time

The Buddha taught that our existence on Earth is a construct of our minds. As such, all we experience in this "form" has no permanence. To explain this, the Buddha adopted, as he did for all his teachings, a dual point of view, one pragmatic and evident and one scientific or hypothesized. For instance, if we talk about the lifetime of a chair, we discuss it in terms of its actual tangible presence. With little effort we can find or represent a chair in our presence. This is pragmatic. When we say that at one point in time, this very chair did not exist, we may or may not be speaking of actual experience and yet we "know" that this chair could not have "existed" before the formation of the planets or the universe itself. It is also true that the demise of this same chair is absolutely certain. We "know" this through the observation of endless other "things" designed, built, aged, and decomposed throughout our environments. Although we may not experience the decomposition and disappearance of this particular chair in our lifetime, we can certainly hypothesize with certainty that at some point, the chair will no longer "exist". This state of "things" also termed Nama Rupa or "Name and Form" is the condition of our existence named "Samsara".

When we speak of Samsara, we speak of things as they appear in this condition of name and form. When we speak of Awakening, or True nature, True entity and such, these are Truths that are permanent and intransient. This is where the first misperception of the Buddha's teachings occurs.

Because the concept of Samsara is a world of total impermanence, and the concept of "Awakening" is a world of permanence, these are taken to mean two separate and distinct "places" or states. In fact, much of the Buddha's teaching trained his followers to perceive the impermanence of their very thoughts and minds. In order that a person understand at a fundamental level that it is the desire or craving one experiences that is the source of suffering, it is very difficult to understand that we control our own suffering. But that is a very immediate and intimate training experience.

For instance, it is relatively easy to say that a chair is impermanent, that there is no True Entity called chair. But try not to utter a sound or word for a month. Six months. At first it is a major annoyance to be unable to communicate. Then it becomes a frightening experience of not being known by others and so on. At some point you quell the desire for conversation, then quell fears of being known, and so on. At the end of this experiment, one understands the relationship and complexities driving the "need" for speech. And, one suffers much less as a result of appeasing those urges for speech. But the connection from this learning to understanding that Samsara itself is the same such a construct is a much greater task. Also, a fundamental of the teachings is easily missed here. For it is not that Samsara is to be dissolved or that Enlightenment is the escape from Samsara per say, but that Enlightenment exists within Samsara and that Samsara is a tool to assist in the attainment of Enlightenment.

To put it another way, as Einstein's equation so eloquently states, "E=Mc^2", Energy is simply matter at a rate of time. You may recall, "E" is energy, "M" is matter, and "c" is the speed of light. The speed of light is contingent upon there being "space" to be "traveled" over time. Space and Time is in fact the same thing. So follow me in a little thought experiment, as Einstein would call it.

As we know from high school geometry, a point is a non-existent thing, only a reference. It has no depth or width or height lest it become a line or shape (form). And what is a line but the shortest distance between two points. A line is only "distance" (space/time), but no form. Even when we intersect the line with another line, all we have done is to define a plane of the distance of the lines. From one "dimension" to two "dimension". Although "time/space" began with the "distance" between two points, "form" cannot exist until we have three dimensions. We have been playing with time/space for a very long time...

Now picture yourself floating high above a major city. The city "forms" are defined by height, width, length, depth, geography, topology, etc... Take a moment to catalogue the immense diversity of different "things" you see. The noises, shouting, discord, passions, desires, cravings; the cars, buildings, restaurants, people, animals, trees, etc... Now imagine that you are able to flatten this entire "reality" into one flat plane. Flatten all the physical as well as emotional "things". Do you still see different "things"? If so, flatten it ten thousand times over, until every "thing" is crushed into infinitely small particles of dust spanning as far as the eye can see. Continue to crush until every "thing" is so finely pulverized that no discernable shape or reference to form exists down to two-dimensional space. Emotions and cars are intermixed and indiscernible. At this point in our thought experiment in pragmatic reasoning, we might say that there is no longer any form called building, or car, or craving, love, addiction; but we can also reason that every "thing" that we have pulverized still remains as energies with particular potentials to manifest certain tendencies and conditions that can interact with one another should there be any "volition" to do so, within this highly homogenized soup we have created. This is in fact Einstein's law of the "conservation of matter" that states that matter can never be destroyed but instead takes on different form or becomes energy. It might also help to visualize this "soup" of potentials and energy to be unstable on a gargantuan scale.

Picture if you will this immense flattened plane of no thickness as we have just created it, stretching out in all directions to infinity. Now, as you envision this massive, transparent collection of energy and potentials reaching out beyond imagination, instantly visualize it collapse into an infinitesimal point directly in front of you, only to explode wildly into the massive potential it was less than a second ago and continue repeating this until you can see this potential eternal energies in as state of constant awareness and quiescence, in both states, at the same "time". This is the state of Wuji, or Grand Ultimate. It is a state of no differentiation (no name and form). This is a state of myriad and countless potentials only. Because here there is no time, for there is no dimension. This would resemble the state from which this universe was manifested. These potential energies diffuse and dispersed as they might be, should some of these potentials attract or combine to perceive or interact, could simply do so by desiring to give rise to tendencies or conditions and thereby begin a motive force or "will". And thus desire or craving of some of these potentials will bring about the chain of actions to aggregate a new version of form, shaping time/space along with it.

In its state as formlessness, these energies, this mixture of potentials, all is calm and free from tribulations or suffering. From the moment when tendencies, conditions and cravings aggregate, and the potentials begin to manifest, the suffering intrinsically begins. Cravings are insatiable, and by nature simply give rise constantly to more cravings, and this is suffering.

This is the first Great truth of the Buddha's teachings. "All existence is suffering."

Shakyamuni

Siddhārtha Gautama - spiritual teacher in the north eastern region of the Indian subcontinent who founded Buddhism. In most Buddhist traditions, he is regarded as the Supreme Buddha (Sammāsambuddha) of our age, "Buddha" meaning "awakened one" or "the enlightened one", or the "Thus Gone One". The time of his birth and death are uncertain: most early 20th-century historians dated his lifetime as c. 563 BCE to 483 BCE

Fundamentals

The Four Noble Truths are often cited as the first fundamental teaching of the Buddha. Little time is adequately afforded to the meaning of this teaching however. The Four Noble Truths are as follows:

1) All existence is suffering

2) All suffering is caused by selfish cravings

3) Eradication of all selfish cravings brings about cessation of all suffering and gives rise to nirvana (liberation from all suffering)

4) The way of ceasing all selfish cravings to extinguish all suffering is the Eightfold Path

Well, let us review each of these one at a time to better understand the teachings encapsulated in these seemingly straightforward statements.

Firstly, "All existence is suffering" is strictly a "pragmatic" statement in reference to "existence" in the state or condition of Samsara. As we learned in the previous chapter on "Time", there is eternal or true existence, and there is also existence in the condition of Nama-Rupa or Name and Form. We also learned that it is the tendencies and conditions, energies that by themselves are inert, but when attracted by desire or craving to other energies can aggregate and give rise to Nama-Rupa and bring about a Samsaric condition of "existence". It can be reasoned by this process that Samsaric existence can only come about by a process of cravings or desires leading to manifestation in name and form. When we speak of "desire" or "craving" it is important to understand that all such energy (craving is an energy) is by its very nature an insatiable condition. So it follows that insatiable conditions are the cause of all suffering. Crave love, receive it and only want more. Crave food, receive it and crave dessert, then relief, then more food, and so on. It may seem that we in Samsara are able to "satisfy" our desires, but the fact is that desire and craving are never satisfied. It is only our minds, our egos that play at satisfaction or accomplishment. We are always attendant to our desire. And since, in pragmatic reasoning, desires can never be realized, is it not a simple observation to state that all existence (pragmatic existence) is suffering?

Secondly, "All suffering is caused by selfish cravings" is simply a restating of the first noble truth. This statement though is not only pragmatic as the first truth is. Where the first noble truth takes its position as firmly within the Samsaric realm, this second truth starts in pragmatic "suffering" but then extends its cause just beyond Samsara to its formative progenitors of cravings.

If one studies the Buddha's teaching of the 12 linked chain of causation, called the 12 Nibanna or Nidanna in Pali, the trace of energies from the grand ultimate of potentials that begin to react and cluster are defined in twelve steps leading to Samsara, birth, old age, sickness, and death. But, as to death we must be clear that the Buddha never taught of reincarnation. This is a very misunderstood aspect of the Buddha's teaching. The Buddha spoke of lifetimes. These "lifetimes" are pragmatic to Samsara. True existence has no time. So the term "life-time" has no meaning other than manifestations of aggregate potentials within Samsara. One's lifetime does not carry over into the grand ultimate and re-manifest again within Samsara, in any form, as we are about to understand. And this brings us to the Third Noble Truth, "Eradication of all selfish cravings brings about cessation of all suffering and gives rise to nirvana (liberation from all suffering)".

We are "born" in this physical manifestation by virtue of tendencies and conditions of energies combining constantly by force of will (volition) to be what and who we are. There is no particle or molecule or energy named Chuck. Chuck is not manifest of previous Chucks, nor does Chuck enter death as a bag of tendencies and conditions and cravings named Chuck. Everything Chuck does, thinks, or says is a function of what Chuck "wants" to "be". Further, what Chuck "wants to be" is only a function of the selfish cravings that assembled to give rise to Chuck. But, Chuck never gets there. Chuck, like you and I, never fully becomes Chuck. We have moments, sometimes, only to be followed immediately by more to do, say, think, be. This is why Buddhists speak of living in a state of "becoming". We truly never "are", because our egos, our will to "be", our "selfish cravings" never ever cease. And so it follows that in death, there is no Chuck either, or you or I. In death, those tendencies and conditions that gave rise to a "self" / "ego" that we have constantly added to, deviated from and been influenced by, simply dis-aggregate and are reabsorbed into the grand ultimate of potentials.

It is important to note that as we have lived "our" lives, we have essentially only reacted to and imprinted more cravings and tendencies that, at death add to the potentials and energies contained in the grand ultimate much as the streams and rivers flow back into the oceans with traces of their journeys down the mountains and lands they flowed through.

The Fourth Noble Truth is more an exegesis and totally pragmatic. "The way of ceasing all selfish cravings to extinguish all suffering is the Eightfold Path" directs us to a "way of living" our Samsaric lives in such a way as to train our minds, and egos through the appeasement of all of our tendencies and therefore selfish cravings. The message here is not one of asceticism per say, unless that is what you feel you must do in order to control your tendencies, but instead a guide to understanding the forces at work in your life and the root cause of your suffering.

The eightfold Path is:

1) Right views
2) Right thinking
3) Right speech
4) Right action
5) Right way of life
6) Right endeavor
7) Right mindfulness
8) Right meditation

Early on in the Buddha's teaching life, the people he lived around knew very little about these ideas. In fact I would challenge anyone today to write a concise definition and outline of training to accomplish these eight life paths. So in his day, the Buddha had to spend many years teaching these paths in order that the populace could begin to understand what is meant to live in a "right" way. All those teachings were never the stated goal of the Buddha though there exist today a plethora of Buddhist sects who still think that the way to enlightenment is through these early teachings. What a sorrowful footnote to the limitations of the ego and the tendencies of Samsaric life. The Buddha is lamenting this I am certain.

Ultimate Teaching

In the last eight years of his Samsaric life the Buddha taught that the method to enlightenment or Buddhahood was quite simple, and yet very difficult to understand. To attain Buddhahood in this lifetime was simple, because it would only require regular and repeatable action which he outlined and defined, and difficult because it would require complete conviction without complete comprehension.

It was not until 1,500 years after the Buddha's passing that a Chinese scholar by the name of Chih-che also known as Chih-I and later adopting the name of the grand mountain on which his school of Buddhism was built (a custom of the times) of T'ien-T'ai that the proper importance was given to this teaching. The people of the Buddha's day were simply incapable of understanding the simplicity of the ultimate practice for enlightenment. Even Chi-I, although elucidating the entire Buddhist canon, and the significance of the title, the sound, and the depth of meaning within the title of this specific sutra, was unable to grasp it as the only means by which to attain enlightenment.

What Chih-I was to demonstrate and definitively explain would be the nature and significance of the Characters used to title each chapter and the entirety of the Teaching of the Wondrous Lotus Flower. These characters were shown to contain every nuance and aspect of all the Buddha's teachings. From the sound of the intonation of each character down to the individual concepts transmitted in each stroke of the characters and the meaning of each independently as well as in the specific combination of the sequence of the characters, Chih-I showed the title was in fact the composite of all of the Buddha's teaching life. Further that the implicit meaning of the title characters was the roadmap and the explicit statement that all sentient beings already possess enlightenment and that it is to be awakened in this current life. Samsara and eternity are simply two sides of the same coin. The coin in this simile represents the life force or essence or potential of all phenomena and noumena.

That was pretty radical thinking at the time, and it was not until much later in Japan in the Shogunate period of the 13th century, about 2,000 years after the Buddha's passing that a priest named Nichiren was able to explicitly announce the Buddha's intent.

Even then, the Buddha had foreseen that it would not be until 2500 years after his passing that the true teachings would begin to flourish throughout the world. And it is now the purpose of this book that I write with all the clarity I can, the true intent and simple teachings of the Buddha as practice in Quantum Life Buddhism. Quantum, because as you have already read, the "reality" of time/space, and the behavior of all phenomena described by the Buddha are exactly as we can observe in Quantum; Life, because the Buddha's teachings are a scientific and complete methodology to live a happy and enlightened life in Samsara and for eternity.

The Buddha taught throughout his teaching years that there are three fundamental aspects of daily life required to attain enlightenment. It was not until Nichiren's elucidation of the Lotus Sutra building upon T'ien-T'ai, Dengyo, Miao-Lo, Vasubandhu, and Nagarjuna, that it becomes all-inclusive in the recitation of the Daimoku. As is shown in later chapters, enlightenment is available at any and all moments of life, but to maintain it then becomes the goal of this Samsaric lifetime. The three fundamental aspects of Buddhist practice remain:

Deep Understanding

The Buddha taught that deep understanding is essential to any endeavor, and no less so to life. To understand means to study, and the Buddha exhorted his disciples and followers to study not only Buddhist teachings, but also all teachings, because ultimately, all teachings are Buddhist.

Deep Practice

The Buddha taught that practice must not be merely rote or superficial. In order that Buddhist Practice is meaningful and successful, one must understand what and why one is doing something. In this way, strong practice is the sibling of deep understanding through study and meditation.

Awakening

The Buddha taught that all his teachings were in the goal that all sentient beings would have the tools and ability to attain enlightenment in their current form and in this lifetime. This would be achieved through deep conviction that could only be achieved through deep practice and deep understanding. This deep conviction was taught to be of the greatest importance, since only deep conviction was capable of bringing about understanding and deep practice, whereas the other two could not by themselves achieve Awakening. Some have translated this as "faith". However, faith does not accurately represent the Buddha's teaching, since faith has a strong component of waiting for and being bequeathed some gift or power from outside one's life. This always leads to the implicit need of a savior or outside source for the enlightenment that the practitioner is awaiting to have bestowed upon them. In True Buddhism, by the word of the Buddha's teachings, it is transliterated in several ways throughout his teaching life as follows:

- Having a strong mind
- Awakening of innate Buddha-nature
- Never looking outside one's self
- Completely dedicated
- Determined
- Single mindedly determined

And there are many longer quotes from the Buddha's teachings that make obvious the true intent of his teachings. There is no need of mystic sources of enlightenment or praying, asking, bequeathing, or even to search and find. The source of enlightenment is not even a "source". Enlightenment, or Buddhahood, simply "is", and is simply obfuscated by the veils of illusions, delusions, and the carnival of misperceptions created by our sense of self, our egos, manifest by our tendencies and selfish cravings.

Nagarjuna

(c. 150 - 250 CE) Indian Philosopher

Reaffirmation

Nagarjuna was a great Indian scholar who dedicated his life to the correct transmission of the Buddha's teachings. During his lifetime (150-250 CE) Nagarjuna saw many misinterpretations of fundamental concepts of the Buddha's teachings. One predominant misunderstanding was of the concept of Anatman or No-self-nature that we have already touched upon in our discussion of the impermanence of all phenomena.

In Nägärjuna's Mulamadhyamakakarika (Verses from the Center); English Translation by Stephen Batchelor; he makes the following argument regarding the "self":

Investigation of Self and Things
(Self)

1. If the aggregates were self, it would be possessed of arising and decaying. If it were other than the aggregates, it would not have the characteristics of the aggregates.

2. If the self did not exist, where could what is mine exist? In order to pacify self and what is mine, grasping I and grasping mine can exist no more.

3. The one who does not grasp at me and mine likewise does not exist.

Whoever sees the one who does not grasp at me and mine does not see.

4. When one ceases thinking of inner and outer things as self and mine, clinging will come to a stop. Through that ceasing, birth will cease.

5. Through the ceasing of action and affliction, there is freedom. Action and affliction [come] from thoughts and they from fixations. Fixations are stopped by emptiness.

6. It is said that "there is a self," but "non-self" too is taught. The Buddhas also teach there is nothing which is "neither self nor non-self."

7. That to which language refers is denied, because an object experienced by the mind is denied. The unborn and unceasing nature of reality is comparable to nirvana.

8. Everything is real, not real; both real and not real; neither not real nor real: this is the teaching of the Buddha.

9. Not known through others, peaceful, not fixed by fixations, without conceptual thought, without differentiation: these are the characteristics of Suchness.

10. Whatever arises dependent on something else is at that time neither that very thing nor other than it. Hence it is neither severed nor permanent.

11. That ambrosial teaching of the Buddhas, those guardians of the world, is neither the same nor different, neither severed nor permanent.

[Buddhapalita commentary: Not the same, not different, not severed, and not permanent - that is the ambrosial teaching of the Buddha, the guardian of the world.]

12. When perfect Buddhas do not appear, and when their disciples have died out, the wisdom of the self-awakened ones will vividly arise without reliance.

It may take some time to discover the logic and brilliant construct of these statements. There is a great deal more as well. It can be derived from just this small portion of the Mulamadhyamakakarika that the "self" has no true nature, or that there is no "self-nature". As discussed earlier, the impermanence of all phenomena is a core teaching of the Buddha. In Quantum too we observe that matter at its most base level is observable as both wave of energy or particle of mass, and as neither particle or wave until observed. This is exactely what the Buddha taught as the true nature of the Samsaric world, our universe. What Nagarjuna was famous for doing was to reverse the argument in order to make it more transparant and evident to understand. Instead of trying to convince you that a person with the name John has no self-nature, but is merely a construct, impermanent and fleeting, Nagarjuna would begin by asking "what if John were permanent and thereby have a self-nature?" If John is a self-natured "entity", then there is no need for John to be born or to die. There would simply always be John. And all things would or could be measured in the degree of John-ness. However, since we know that John is born, and does die, we can observe that there is no John-ness nor is there any permanence or self-nature that is John. John is given rise to by aggregates of tendencies and conditions as an instance or instantiation of an ever evolving set of tendencies, which themselves are subject of change at every "moment".

Vasubandhu

4th century Buddhist scholar

The following is excerpt from an excellent book by Stefan Anacker titled "Seven Works of Vasubandhu".

A Discussion of the Five Aggregates

(PANCASKANDHAKA-PRAKARANA)

Homage to Manjusri-kumāra-bhūta₁

1. The five aggregates are the aggregate of materialities, the aggregate of feelings, the aggregate of cognitions, the aggregate of motivational dispositions, and the aggregate of consciousnesses.

What is *materiality?'* Materiality is whatever has dimensionality, and consists of all of the four great elements, and everything that is derived from the four great elements. And what are the four great elements? They are the earth-element, water-element, fire-element, and wind-element. Among these, what is the earth-element? It is solidity. What is the water-element? It is liquidity. What is the fire-element? It is heat. What is the wind-element? It is gaseousness. What is derived from them? The sense-organ of the eye, the sense-organ of the ear, the sense-organ of the nose, the sense-organ of the tongue, the sense-organ of the body, visibles, sounds, smells, tastes, everything that can be subsumed under tactile sensations, and un-manifest action. And among these, what is the sense-organ of the eye? It is sentient materiality, which has color as its sense-object.

What is the sense-organ of the ear? It is sentient materiality, which has sounds as its sense-object. What is the sense-organ of the nose? It is sentient materiality, which has smells as its sense-object. What is the sense-organ of the tongue? It is sentient materiality, which has tastes as its sense-object. What is the sense-organ of the body? It is sentient materiality, which has tactile sensations as its sense-object. And what are visibles? They are the sense-objects of the eye: color, configuration, and manifest action. And what are sounds? They are the sense-objects of the ear, having as their causes great elements appropriated by the body, or great elements un-appropriated. And what are smells? They are the sense-objects of the nose: pleasant smells, unpleasant smells, and those, which are neither. And what are tastes? They are the sense-objects of the tongue: sweet, sour, salty, sharp, bitter, and astringent. What is everything that can be subsumed under tactile sensations? They are the sense-objects of the body: the great elements themselves, softness, hardness, heaviness, lightness, coldness, hunger, and thirst. What is un-manifest action? It is materiality, which has arisen from manifest action or meditational concentration: it is invisible and exercises no resistance.

2. And what *are feelings?* They are experiences, and are of three kinds: pleasure, suffering, and that which is neither pleasure nor suffering. Pleasure is whatever there arises a desire to be connected with again, once it has stopped. Suffering is whatever there arises a desire to be separated from, once it has arisen. That which is

neither pleasure nor suffering is whatever towards which neither desire arises, once it has arisen.

3. And what are *cognitions?* They are the grasping of signs in a sense-object. They are of three kinds: indefinite, definite, and immeasurable. Gunaprabhain his *Pancaskandha-vivarana* explains "immeasurable cognitions" as follows: one can have a cognition of immeasurability, of space, of the ocean, etc.

4. And what are *motivational dispositions?* They are events associated with cittas,[7] other than feelings and cognitions, and those that are disassociated from cittas. Among these, what are the events associated with cittas? They are whatever events are associated with cittas. And what are they? They are contact, mental attention, feelings, cognitions, volitions, zest, confidence, memory or mindfulness, meditational concentration, insight, conviction, inner shame, dread of blame, the root-of-the-beneficial of lack of greed, the root-of-the-beneficial of lack of hostility, the root-of-the-beneficial of lack of confusion, vigor, tranquility, carefulness, equanimity, attitude of non-harming, attachment, aversion, pride, ignorance, views, doubt, anger, malice, hypocrisy, maliciousness, envy, selfishness, deceitfulness, guile, mischievous exuberance, desire to harm, lack of shame, lack of dread of blame, mental fogginess, excited-ness, lack of conviction, sloth, carelessness, loss of mindfulness, distractedness, lack of recognition, regret, torpor, initial mental application, and subsequent discursive thought.

Among these, the first five occur in every citta. The next five are certain only with specific objects-of-sense. The next eleven are beneficial. The next six are afflictions.

The rest are secondary afflictions. The last four also become different (i.e. they are capable of being either afflictions or beneficial).

And what is *contact?* It is the distinguishing, which comes after the three (sense-organ, object-of-sense, and corresponding consciousness) have met together. And what is *mental attention?* It is the entering into done by a citta. What is *volition?* It is mental action, which impels a citta towards good qualities, flaws, and that, which is neither. And what is *zest?* It is desire towards a range of events of which there is consciousness. And what is *confidence?* It is holding to certainty in regard to a range of events of which there is certainty. What is *memory?* It is the non-forgetting of a range of events towards which there is acquaintance, and is a certain kind of discourse of citta. What is *meditational concentration?* It is one-pointed-ness of citta towards an examined range of events. What is *insight?* ? It is discernments as regards the same, and is either understanding, that which has arisen from not having understood, or that which is different from these two. What *is conviction?* It is firm conviction, desire, and serenity of citta towards action, its results, the beneficial, and the Gems. What is *inner shame?* It is a shame coming about through a committed offense, in which the self, or rather the (psychological) event responsible, is predominant. And what is *dread of blame?* It is that shame towards others that comes about through a committed offense, in which the outer world is predominant. What is *lack of greed?* It is the antidote to greed, a non-attachment to that which is arising in Manas. What is *lack of hostility?* It is the antidote to hostility, and is loving-kindness. What is *lack of confusion?* It is the antidote to confusion, and is right recognition. And what is *vigor?* It is the antidote to sloth, and is enthusiasm of citta towards the beneficial. And what is *tranquility?* It is the antidote to a situation of susceptibility to harm, and is a skill in bodily and mental action. And what is *carefulness?* It is the antidote to carelessness, a cultivation of those beneficial events which are antidotes, and abandoning unbeneficial events through continuing in those beneficial factors: lack of greed, up to vigor. What is *equanimity?* It is whatever evenness of citta, remaining in a tranquil state of citta, total tranquility in citta continuing in those factors-lack of greed up to vigor, through which there is continuity in a state without afflictions through the clearing away of afflicted events. And what is an *attitude of non-harming?* It is the antidote to an attitude of harming, and is compassion. And what is *attachment!* It is adherence to any fixed intent in appropriating aggregates. And what is *aversion?* It is a tormented volition towards sentient beings. And what is *pride?* There are seven kinds of pride: basic pride, greater pride, the pride that is more than pride, the pride of thinking "I am", conceit, the pride of thinking deficiency, and false pride. Basic pride is any inflation of citta, which considers, through smallness, either "I am greater", or "I am equal". What is greater pride? Greater pride is any inflation of citta, which considers, through an equality, that "I am greater" or "I am endowed with greatness." And what is pride that is more than pride? It is any inflation of citta, which considers, through a greatness, that "I am great". And what is the pride of thinking "I am"? It is any inflation of citta, which is connected with the view of either "I am" or "mine" in regard to appropriating aggregates. And what is conceit?

It is any inflation of citta, which considers, in regard to an excellence, which was previously obtained, in another moment, but is no longer, "I've attained it." And what is the pride of thinking deficiency? It is any inflation of citta, which considers, "I am only a little bit inferior to those of greatly excellent qualities." And what is false pride? It is any inflation of citta which considers "I am endowed with good qualities" when good qualities have not been acquired. And what is *ignorance?* It is lack of knowledge regarding action, results of action, the Truths, and the Gems, and also the mentally constructed that rises together with it. In the realm of desires, there are three roots-of-the-unbeneficial: attachment, aversion, and ignorance, and these are the same as the roots-of-the unbeneficial greed, hostility, and confusion. And what are *views?* These views are generally of five kinds: the view of a fixed self in the body, views regarding the permanence or impermanence of the elements constituting personality, false views, adherence to particular views, and adherence to mere rule and ritual. And what is the view of a fixed self in the body? It is an afflicted judgment viewing either an " I " or "mine" in the appropriating aggregates. And what are *views regarding the permanence or the impermanence of the elements constituting personality?* They relate to these same elements (the appropriating aggregates), and are afflicted judgments viewing them as either lasting or discontinuous. And what are *false views?* They are any afflicted judgments, which involve fear towards the elements of existence, and which cast aspersions on the efficacy of cause and effect. What is *adherence to particular views?* It is any afflicted judgment viewing these same three views, and the aggregates, which continue in them, as being the best, the most excellent, attained, and most exalted. And what is *attachment to mere rules and rituals?* It is any afflicted judgment seeing in rules and rituals, and in the aggregates continuing in them, purity, liberation, and a leading to Nirvana. And what is *doubt?* It is any two-mindedness as regards the Truths, etc. The latter three of those afflicted views mentioned above, and doubt, are the basic mentally constructed. The rest of these views are the mentally constructed that often arise together with those. What is *anger?* It is any tormented volition of citta, which all of a sudden becomes intent on doing harm. What is *malice?* It is taking hold of a hostility. What is *hypocrisy? It* is unwillingness to recognize one's/own faults. What is *maliciousness?* It is being enslaved by unpleasant speech. What is *envy?* It is an agitation of citta at the attainments of another. What is *selfishness?* It is a holding fast to a citta, which is not in accord with giving. What is *deceitfulness?* It is attempting to show forth to another an unreal object through an action of decoying. What is *guile?* It is a deceitfulness of citta, which seizes an opportunity for making secret one's own flaws. What is *mischievous exuberance?* It is holding fast to a delighted citta unconnected with internal good qualities. What is an *attitude of harming?* It is an intention unbeneficial towards sentient beings. And what is *lack of shame?* It is a lack of internal shame at offences one has committed. And what is *lack of dread of blame?* It is a lack of dread towards others at offences one has committed. What is *mental fogginess?* It is a lack of skill in mental action, and is thick-headedness. What is *excited-ness?* It is lack of calm in citta. What is *lack of conviction?* It is a lack of trust in a citta, which is not in accord with conviction, towards action and its results the Truths and the Gems. What is *sloth?* It is a lack of enthusiasm towards the beneficial in a citta, and is that which is not in accord with vigor. What is *carelessness?* It is any non-guarding of citta from afflictions, and non-cultivation of the beneficial, which comes about by being linked with greed, hostility, confusion, or sloth. What is *loss of mindfulness?* It is an afflicted mindfulness, an un-clarity as to the beneficial. What is *distractedness?* It is any diffusion of citta, which partakes of greed, hostility, or confusion on the five sense-qualities of the realm of desires. What is *lack of recognition?* It is a judgment connected with afflictions, by which there is entry into not knowing what body, voice, or Manas have done. What is *regret?* It is remorse, a piercing sensation in Manas. What is *torpor"?* It is a contraction of citta, which is without capacity for entering down into anything. What is *initial mental application'?* A discourse of inquiry by Manas, a certain kind of volition and discernment, which can be characterized as an indistinct state of citta. What is *(subsequent) discursive thought?* A discourse of examination by Manas, which in the same way can be characterized as a more precise state of citta.

And what are the *motivating dispositions disassociated from cittas?* These are pure designations for situations in materialities, cittas, and events associated with cittas, and are designations only for these, and not for anything else. And what are they? *Präpti,* the attainment without cognitions, the attainment of the cessation of cognitions and feelings, any non-meditative state without cognitions, life-force, taking part in an organism, birth, decrepitude, continuity, lack of duration, the collection of words, the collection of phrases, the collection of syllables, the state of being separate from Dharma, and other factors like these.

Among these, what is *präpti?* It is becoming connected with something attained. Actually, it is a "seed", a capacity, an approachment, and an adjustment to circumstances. And what is *an attainment free from cognitions?* It is any cessation of non-stable events: cittas and events associated with cittas, which is totally clear and separate from attainments, and which comes about through a mental attention dispensing with cognitions about to arise, where former cognitions do not exist. And what is *the attainment of the cessation of cognitions and feelings?* It is any cessation of non-stable and more stable events, cittas and events associated with cittas, which comes about through a mental attention dispensing with cognitions, continuing in which comes after the summits of existence have been practiced, and which is separate even from those attainments present in the stage-of-nothing-whatever. And what is a *non-meditative state without cognitions?* It is the cessation of non-stable events: cittas and events associated with cittas, which takes place, for instance, within those groups of gods which are sentient, but do not have cognitions. What is *life-force?* It is, as regards any events taking part in an organism, any continuity, for a certain time, of motivating dispositions, which have been projected by past action. And what is *taking part in an organism?* It is any close interrelationship of bodily parts as regards sentient beings. What is *birth?* It is any arising of a stream of motivating dispositions, which has not already arisen, as regards any collection of events taking part in an organism. And what is *decrepitude?* It is an alteration in the stream of those like that (i.e. events taking part in an organism). What is *continuity?* It is the serial propagation in the stream of those like that. What is *lack of duration?* It is the discontinuity in the stream of those like that. What is the *collection of words?* It is denotations for the own-beings of events. What is the *collection of phrases?* It is denotations for the particularities of events. What is the *collection of syllables?* They are the syllables of actual sound through which the other two are disclosed. Though these all refer to speech, meanings are communicated dependent on words and phrases. For the same syllable does not arise with another synonym. And what is the *state of being separate from Dharma?* It is the non-attainment of noble psychological events.

These all are called "the aggregate of motivational dispositions".

5. And what is *consciousness?* It is awareness of an object-of-consciousness; visibles, etc. "Citta" and "Manas" are the same as consciousness. They are so designated because of their variety, and because of their providing a mental basis, respectively. Actually, the store consciousness is also citta, as it accumulates the seeds for all motivating dispositions. It is objects-of-consciousness and aspects are un-discerned. It joins an assemblage pertaining to an organism into a felt relationship, and continues as a series of moment-events. Thus, though there is awareness of a sense-object immediately upon emerging from the attainment of cessation of cognitions and feelings, the attainment free from cognitions, or a non-meditative state without cognitions, it arises as the consciousness of the attainments themselves; it is the state of evolvement into

another aspect once there has been perception dependent upon any object-of-consciousness; it is the state of citta's arising again even after the consciousness-stream has been severed; it is entry into Samsära and transmigration in it. This same store-consciousness is the support of all the seeds, the basis and causality for the body, and the state of continuance in a body. It is also called "the appropriating consciousness", because it appropriates a body. Used in the sense of a specific entity, *Manas* is an object-of-consciousness, within the store-consciousness, a consciousness always connected with confusion of self, the view of a self, pride of self, love of self, etc. It also joins an assemblage pertaining to an organism into a felt relationship, and continues as a series of moment-events, but does not exist in a saint, the Noble Path, or at the time of the attainment of cessation.

Why are the aggregates thus designated? It is through their collectivity, i.e. various kinds of materialities, etc., being heaped up together that "times", "series", "aspects", "developments", and "sense-objects" seem to occur.

The twelve *sense-fields* are the sense-field of the eye and the sense-field of visibles, the sense-field of the ear and the sense-field of sounds, the sense-field of the nose and the sense-field of smells, the sense-field of the tongue and the sense-field of tastes, the sense-field of the body and the sense-field of tactile sensations, the sense-field of *Manas* and the sense-field of mentally cognizables. The eye, visibles, the ear, sounds, the nose, smells, the tongue, tastes have all been discussed previously. The sense-field of the tactile is the four great elements and everything (all the incredibly numerous various sensations), which can be subsumed under tactile sensations. The sense-field-of *Manas* are any aggregate of consciousness. The sense-field of mentally cognizables is feelings, cognitions, motivating dispositions, un-manifest action, and the uncompounded. And what is *the uncompounded?* Space, the cessation not through contemplation, the cessation through contemplation, and Such-ness. Among these, what is *space?* It is any interval separating materialities. What is *a cessation not through contemplation?* It is any non-separation from cessation without antidotes to afflictions figuring in. And what is *cessation through contemplation?* It is any non-separation from cessation, any constant non-arising of aggregates through antidotes to afflictions. What is *Suchness?* It is the "inherent nature *(dharmata)* of any event", and is the selflessness of events.

Why are these called *"sense-fields"?* Because they are the doors to the rising of consciousness. The eighteen *sensory domains* are the domain of the eye, the domain of the visible, the domain of the visual consciousness; the domain of the ear, the domain of sounds, the domain of audial consciousness; the domain of the nose, the domain of smells, the domain of olfactory consciousness; the domain of the tongue, the domain of tastes, the domain of gustatory consciousness; the domain of the body, the domain of the tactile, the domain of tactile consciousness, the domain of the *Manas,* the domain of mentally cognizables, and the domain of the mental consciousness. The domains of the eye, etc., and the domains of visibles, etc., are the same as the sense-fields. The domains of the six consciousnesses are awarenesses with objects-of-consciousness in visibles, etc., and which are dependent on the eye, etc. The domain of *Manas* is any of these consciousness-moments which are past immediately afterwards, because of the continuity of the sixth consciousness. In this way, the sensory domains have been determined as eighteen.

Ten of those sense-fields and domains (the sensory organs and their objects) and that part of the sense-field of mentally cognizables, which may be subsumed under it (un-manifest action) constitute whatever is the aggregate of materiality. The sense-field of *Manas* and the seven domains of citta (the visual, olfactory, gustatory, tactile, and mental consciousnesses, and the domain of mentally cognizables) constitute whatever is the aggregate of consciousness. The sense-fields and domains of mentally cognizables also constitute whatever are the other three aggregates (feelings, cognitions, and motivating dispositions), one part of the aggregate of materiality, which may be subsumed under it (un-manifest action), and the uncompounded. Why are these called "domains"? It is because they grasp a "characteristic", though without a "doer". As to why they are called *"aggregates", etc.*, this serves as an antidote to the three kinds of grasping after self, in order. The three kinds, of grasping after self are grasping for one central entity, grasping for an "enjoyer", and grasping for a "doer".

Among these eighteen sensory domains, which contain materiality? Whatever has the own-being of the aggregate of materiality. Which do not contain materiality? The rest of them. Which can be seen? Only the sensory domain of visibles is an object-of-sense, which can be seen. Which are invisible? The rest of them. Which exercise resistance? The ten, which contain materiality, which exercise resistance on each other. Which do not exercise resistance? The rest of them. Which are liable to be connected with afflictions? Fifteen (i.e. the sensory domains of the eye to tactile consciousness), and part of the last three *(manas,* mentally cognizables, and mental consciousness). Which are un-liable to be connected with afflictions? Part of the last three. Those because of having a scope allowing for the direct perception of the arising of afflictions. Which are without afflictions? Part of the last three. Which occur, in the realm of desires? All of them. Which occur in the realm of simple images? Fourteen : all of them except smells, tastes, olfactory-consciousness, and gustatory-consciousness. Which occur in the imageless sphere?" Part of the last three. Which are included within the aggregates? All of them except the uncompounded. Which are included within the appropriating aggregates? Those constituting a "personality". Which are beneficial, which unbeneficial, and which indeterminate? Ten may belong to any of the three categories: the seven sensory domains of citta, and the sensory domains of visibles, sounds and mentally cognizables. The rest of them are all indeterminate. Which are "internal"? Twelve of them: all of them except visibles, sounds, smells, tastes, tactile sensations and mentally cognizables. Which are "external"? Six of them: those not included in the preceding. Which have an object-of-consciousness? The seven sensory domains of citta, and one part of the sensory domain of mentally cognizables, namely, whatever events are associated with cittas. Which are without an object-of-consciousness? The ten others and most of the sensory domains of mentally cognizables. Which contain discrimination? The sensory domains of *Manas,* mental consciousness, and mentally cognizables. Which do not contain discrimination? The rest of them. Which are appropriated? Five of the "internal" (organs I-V) and part of the "external" (i.e. part of visibles, sounds, smells, tastes, and tactile sensations). Which are un-appropriated? Part of the four (all visibles, smells, tastes and tactile sensations not integral parts of the sensory organism). Which are functional *(sabhäga)?* The five internal material ones (organs I-V) because there is a correspondence between the specific consciousness and its sensory domain. Which are non-functional *(tat-sabhägä)?* The same when they are empty in relation to their specific consciousness, because of a conformity of each to its own knowledge.

I included this excerpt from the "Seven Works of Vasubandhu" for three reasons. Firstly, this is a great example of the intense scrutiny and scholarship of the sages who dedicated their lives to the correct transmission of the Buddha's teachings. Secondly, though this is but one small example, it is clear that the study and practice of Buddhism involve no mysticism and is totally grounded in observational analysis of an extremely high degree. And Lastly, there is always the question of birth and death in the form of, "where do we come from" and after death, "where do we go", in any discussion of how to properly live one's life. No other system of thought answers these questions without resorting to conjecture at best and mysticism at most. From the above example it is hoped that the analytic and logical reasoning of True Buddhism will have impressed that the question of birth and death, beyond being the basis for all of Buddhism, are thoroughly investigated and defined within the framework of life and eternity. I wish to introduce one more branch of thought before putting a final period at the end of the birth/death cycle discussion.

Taoists and Buddhists

Jingqishen (Essence, Internal energy, Mind)

When Buddhism entered China, it was invariably viewed in comparison to Taoism and Confucius thought. To the Chinese Emperor of the time, and to the people in general, Taoist thought gave structure to the universe as a whole and placed human existence within its reasoning. Confucius thought applied to governance and behavioral correctness. So Buddhism seemed a beautifully tailored amalgam that allowed for daily behavior to mirror and develop further the human synchronicity with the universal whole. Buddhism flourished for a time in Northern China until the Buddhist scholar Bodhidharma (early 5th CE) who had been sent for by the Emperor had lost the favor of the Emperor. Bodhidharma then sought refuge and a place to teach at the Shaolin Temple. There, after finding the monks sick and weak, Bodhidharma melded the Taoist philosophy of the monks with Buddhist and Indian knowledge of the energy channels within the body known as Qi (Chi), or inner energy. From here was developed the Buddhist view of enlightenment using the training of recognition, leading, and manipulating the Qi in order to calm the mind and attain a state free of attachments. You may have guessed by now that this is the foundation of Ch'an Buddhism, better known by its Japanese name, Zen. The problem with Ch'an is its incompleteness and derivation from the Buddha's true teachings. In reality, Zen or Ch'an should never be considered Buddhism. Even the following patriarchs of Ch'an claim that their sacred texts and methods are from a source outside of the Buddha.

Well, you must understand by now that Buddha is not a human or any other "being". Buddha, in fact, is completely outside the realm of "being" which is only found in Samsara. Buddha exists within and without Samsara in time without time. Remember the flattened non-dimensional plane we created several chapters ago? Buddhahood lies everywhere without "being" anywhere. It is like awareness without manifestation. If you find it difficult to visualize this state of Buddhahood, don't feel bad. The Buddha taught that the truth of Buddhahood could only be shared amongst Buddhas. And there again is that duality we discussed early on. Buddhahood is eternal and non-differentiated, but a person (a differentiated thing) can reveal their Buddhahood. So the Buddha's statement of true Buddhahood or enlightenment is truth, but the last part of sharing between "Buddhas" is pragmatic. Make sense?

Before we move on the scholarship and brilliance of Chi-I, let us take a moment to understand the fundamental three energies of the Taoist Chinese medicine, Jingqishen. Jing-Qi-Shen, are the three forms of energy defined in the Taoist philosophy. Jing is the essence or spirit. Qi, as defined earlier is the inner energy, and Shen is the mind or god power. Jing means the essence, the most original and refined part of everything. Jing exists in everything. Sperm is called Jing Zi, which means "Essence of the Son", because it contains the Jing of the father as passed down to son or daughter and becomes the son's Jing. Jing is the original source of every living thing and determines the nature and characteristics of that thing. It is the root of life. This differs from Buddhism in a very important way. Firstly, there is a contradiction in stating that all Jing is received from one's birth parents and then stating that Jing is the original source of all life, unless of course "all life" is limited strictly to Samsara. This would again set up the dichotomy that life and not-life are separate and distinct things. This is specific contradiction to the Buddha's true teaching that there is no difference other than by Samsaric perception. This would easily explain the basic false premise of Ch'an or Zen that enlightenment can only be reached as a negation of "this" in pursuit of a "that". When put in those terms is it not easy to see why Ch'an fails to deliver immediate enlightenment. Ch'an practitioners are still bound by attachments to "this" and "that". It may function as an excellent calming exercise, but it is far removed from the Buddha's goal of simple, universal, guaranteed enlightenment for all sentient beings no matter what station or capacity.

This is also notable in the Taoist definition of Qi, which is the body's energy that comes either from the conversion of the Jing received from the parents or the food you eat and the air you breathe. Once again, the fundamental elements of your existence are tied solely to that which is physically transmitted from ancestry.

Shen is the center of your mind, or the spirit of your being. Your Qi or energy must nourish the Shen in your body.

There is a great deal of reading material in the martial arts and the Chinese medicinal arts regarding these three essential energies, so that I will not go deeper into their workings. Suffice it to say for the purposes of discussion of the true teachings of the Buddha and the practice of Ch'an of Zen, there is a complete disconnect through this path of evolution.

Taoism does contain concepts that would more accurately mirror the Buddha's teachings if one were to connect the Samsaric and human existence to the Taoist functions of the universe. These would be the concepts of Wuji (grand ultimate – non-differentiation), Taiji (will, Volition, motive force), and Qi (heavenly Qi).

There are three different kinds of Qi. There is the Body-Qi within your body; there is Earth-Qi that is the energies that surround us; and Heavenly-Qi that moves and manipulates the Earth-Qi and ultimately down to our Body-Qi.

The symbol for Wuji is both a dot and a closed circle. It is much like the flattened non-dimensional plane we created earlier, where all that can "exist" is in a quiescent state of potentials.

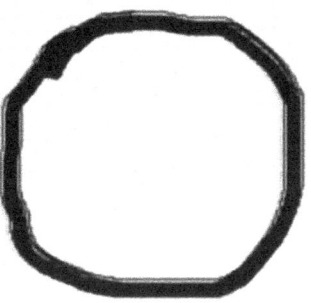

The symbol for Taiji is a spiral, indicating a state of arousal. From this state of arousal, energies are motivated to motion. Many people misinterpret the symbol of Yin/Yang for the concept of Taiji. This is incorrect and demonstrates the deep misunderstanding of the forces at work in all creation. It is like saying that the mere thought of brushing one's teeth results in the teeth being brushed. When, in fact, it is this thought of a desired action that then precipitates the myriad actions involved in moving your body and arms about to locate the tooth brush, the tooth paste, the application of the tooth paste to the brush and so on... Taiji is the "volitional" state.

Once motion is realized, there is differentiation, and so, at this very moment does the Yin/Yang come into being. With differentiation or Yin/Yang, come all "things". Without differentiation, there simply cannot be "thing". Even "action" is a "thing" as it is defined in opposition to in-action.

Chih-I (T'ien-T'ai)

(538–597)

Ichinen Sanzen (3,000 realms in each moment of life)

I have read countless variations on this profound elucidation of the Buddha's teachings first defined in extreme detail by T'ien-T'ai, Chih-i. Most of what is written dissects the mathematics of the 3,000 realms constructed of the concepts of the ten Buddhist worlds or life-states, which, as each world is inclusive of all ten again (i.e. the hell of hell or the realization in animality), results in 10 x 10 or 100. Then multiplied by the ten factors of life rendering 1,000, and finally multiplied by the three realms of existence: of the five components, of living beings, and of the environment. 3 realms multiplied by 1000 and you have 3,000 realms. This may explain the title of this teaching, but does little to tap into the intricate and detailed map of the Buddhas profound jewel of logic and analysis. I will try here to briefly define the components of Ichinen Sanzen, and then to follow but one possible path, just to illustrate the depth of this teaching. I will include complete descriptions in the appendix so to keep this example moving along and trust the names of each of these components will suffice for this exercise. Then I will simplify further in terms we have already used, the implication of this teaching.

The Ten Worlds or life conditions:

1) Hell (anguish, rage)
2) Hunger (insatiable, addictions)
3) Animality (competition, war)
4) Anger (manipulation, subversion, avarice)
5) Tranquility (status quo, resist change)
6) Rapture (temporary elation)
7) Learning (collecting knowledge, able to hear)
8) Realization (applied knowledge, able to see goal)
9) Bodhisattva (facilitator of others to awaken)
10) Buddhahood (awakened)

The Ten Factors of Life: these are attributes common to all phenomena in all of the Ten Worlds termed by the Buddha as "suchnesses".

1) Appearance – (attributes of things discernable from the outside. Color, size, shape, etc...)
2) Nature – (the inherent disposition of a thing or being that cannot be discerned form the outside.)
3) Entity – (the essence of life that permeates and integrates appearance and nature. Jing).
4) Power – (Life's potential energy. Qi)
5) Influence – (the action or movement produced when life's inherent power is activated. Remember Taiji.).

6) Internal cause – (the cause latent in life that produces an effect of the same quality as itself).

7) Relation – (the relationship of indirect causes to internal cause).

8) Latent effect – (the effect produced in life when an internal cause is activated).

9) Manifest effect – (the tangible perceivable result that emerges in time as an expression of latent effect).

10) Consistency from beginning to end - (indicates that all the previous factors must work together at any given moment interrelatedly).

And finally the three realms of existence:

1) The Realm of the Five Components or as stated by Vasubandhu as the Five Aggregates – (analysis of a living entity in terms of how it responds to its surroundings. The five components are: form, perception, conception, volition, and consciousness).

2) The Realm of Living Beings – (the individual living being formed of a temporary union of the five components, who manifests or experiences any of the Ten Worlds.)

3) The Realm of the Environment – (The place of the individual, as well as the reflection of the place and the life condition or world of the place as a function of the individuals' life conditions within it.)

All this is to help the individual understand the depth of the workings of one's life, its origins, and ultimately, what one is dealing with when trying to train the mind toward one goal or enlightenment.

So to work this backwards for an example of the Buddhist conception of the influences and tendencies that give rise to our life as well as our behaviors, here I go...

Donna's environment is cold, forested, and sparsely populated. Remember that all the other people in the region Donna lives also influence this realm. So there is a tough minded rugged sense of life here.

Donna is also aware that there is a larger world and sometimes dreams of escaping her village for the exciting life of a big city in a warm climate, but quickly buries this fantasy and cannot allow herself to manifest the simple acts that could allow her to go, due to the influence of the life conditions surrounding her (which are manifestation of her own life condition). This is the struggle within Donna of the five components shifting constantly and thereby vulnerable to influence.

Donna continues to make internal causes to escape. Her volition motivates small actions that are immediately influenced by her aggregates and force her to hide her act which then creates more conflicting cause and volition that spontaneously burst in momentum only to be caught, ridiculed and even admonished for such thoughts. She wonders if she wanted to get caught, because it is easier than to carry through and face the opposition. Each thought she has further compounds her cause and effects stream back at her as soon as she thinks them. This is a state of suffering.

Even Donna's appearance changes just as she has these thoughts and others through relation can see them so clearly.

Through this entire experience, Donna's life condition is a rollercoaster from elation at a new idea in rapture to hell and rage at being ridiculed, Animality at hiding her activities, hunger at wanting escape ever more even without any idea of what it might mean.

As Donna settles back into routine her worlds of Animality, anger, and hunger find couplings in to hunger/learning, and animal/realization, just as her little sister walks up and asks, "why do you want to leave me sister?" with her eyes full of tears. To which Donna's entire being shifts in appearance, posture, and life state to Bodhisattva, learning and realization, as she explains to her sister as much as to herself that curiosity and unrest can lead to unhappiness and lack of appreciation for the real gifts one has in life...

I make no claim here to have even scratched the surface of the vast number of shifts, decisions, and influences attending each moment in this story. As an example though, I think it is safe to say that the number of influences and decisions we make in every moment of our lives is incalculable. And that is only the ones we are conscious of. What about all the influences, judgments, habits, moods, desires, etc, operating beneath our radar? What Noam Chomsky refers to as the Pre-Conscious mind.

The simple point here is not to become a master puzzle unraveler or a mathematician, it is simply to understand that in order to achieve anything, let alone achieve Buddhahood, will require of us, deep focus and determination. The idea that "cause" can have latent effect through its consistent repetition is the path to changing and appeasing those original tendencies that gave rise to our current situation. It is further admonition to deepen understanding, study, conviction, and practice.

A deeper point of this teaching is that Ichinen Sanzen (3000 realms in a single thought moment) is eternal, it is the nature of the life process and all phenomena from Nomina. This is a teaching that is both pragmatic and transcends Samsara. Remember again our flattened city, completely non-dimensional and non-differentiated potential. In this non-differentiated potential the ten worlds exist and with them the ten factors, and even, in the form of potential, the three realms of existence. Can you see that we have returned to the 12 link causal chain of causation or birth? Also called, twelve *Nidanna s* or twelve-linked chain of dependent origination. The

Sanskrit word *Nidanna means* cause or cause of existence. The Buddha taught the twelve-linked chain of causation in answer to the question of why people have to experience the sufferings of aging and death. Each link in the chain is a cause that leads to the next. The first link in the chain is ignorance (Sanskrit; *avidya*), which gives rise to (2) action *(Samkara)* (also, volition or karmic action); (3) action causes consciousness *(vijñaana),* or the function to discern; (4) consciousness causes name and form *(Nama Rupa),* or spiritual and material objects of discernment; (5) name and form cause the six sense organs *(shad-ayatana);* (6) the six sense organs cause contact *(sparsha);* (7) contact causes sensation *(Vedanä);* (8) sensation causes desire *(trishna);* (9) desire causes attachment *(Upadana);* (10) attachment causes existence *(Bhava);* (11) existence causes birth *(Jati);* and (12) birth causes aging and death *(Jaramarana).*

So to simplify even further, a birth is not simply the reproduction of offspring. When we spoke earlier of the Taoist conception of Jing as coming from the father to the offspring, the critical error is that the father and mother Jing is melded with the already present Jing of the offspring. In fact, there would be no offspring were there not Jing (essence potential) already motivated (Taiji) aggregating (with Qi) the tendencies and conditions (ten worlds, ten factors, three realms) to manifest into Samsara in via the entry into the fertilized egg (sperm and ovum) to develop in the vehicle of the womb.

Once you can understand that process of coming into being, "Where we come from" is a three way deal of volition and not simply the result of man and woman coitus, you will be much better equipped to understand your life, how to live it, and "Where the 'you' goes" when your body dies.

It is like a drop of rain falling into a crystal clear lake. The disappearance of the drop, like death, leaves an imprint upon the surface of the water in ripples that gradually assimilate into the clear surface of the lake. Meanwhile, the drop itself both disintegrates its "self" as it integrates into the vastness of the lake.

Nichiren

(February 16, 1222 – October 13, 1282) a Buddhist monk living during the Kamakura period in Japan.

After T'ien-t'ai there were other schools of Buddhism that for political or prestige, or financial reasons adopted some of the T'ien-t'ai schools doctrines and manipulated, or cast aside others in order to create "superior" schools and gain favor of the rulers of the day. One example is the "Pure Land" Buddhist school that simply appropriated whatever teachings of T'ien-t'ai gained them credibility, claiming the findings as their own and contorting them to suit their desire to idolatry of the one Buddha name Amitābha (Amida). This sect was also known in Japan in some form as the Nembutsu, which Nichiren proved to be a heretical sect. Fortunately, there were great scholars to whom the insights and treatises of T'ien-t'ai were extremely prized, revered, and studied.

Miao-lo (711–782) (PY Miaole; Jpn Myoraku)

Also known as Chan-jan. The sixth patriarch of the T'ient'ai school in China, in the tradition that counts T'ient'ai as the first patriarch. Another tradition, which regards Nagarjuna as the founder, counts Miao-lo as the ninth patriarch. He is revered as the restorer of the T'ient'ai school. He was called the Great Teacher Miao-lo because he lived at Miao-lo-ssu temple, or the Venerable Ching-hsi (also the Great Teacher Ching-hsi) after his birthplace. Born to a Confucian family, at age twenty Miao-lo studied the doctrine of the T'ient'ai school under its fifth patriarch, Hsyan-lang. In 748 he entered the priesthood. At that time, the Zen (Ch'an), Flower Garland (Hua-yen), Dharma Characteristics (Fa-hsiang), and other schools were flourishing, and the T'ient'ai school was in a slight decline. Miao-lo reasserted the supremacy of the Lotus Sutra and wrote commentaries on T'ient'ai's major works, helping clarify and bring about a revival of interest in the school's teachings. He maintained the superiority of the T'ient'ai teachings over the doctrines of other schools. In his later years, he lived at Kuo-ch'ing-ssu temple and died at Fo-lung Monastery, both on Mount T'ient'ai. His commentaries on T'ient'ai's three major works are titled The Annotations on "The Profound Meaning of the Lotus Sutra," The Annotations on "The Words and Phrases of the Lotus Sutra," and The Annotations on "Great Concentration and Insight."

Saichō (最澄) (767–822)

was later to recognize the depth and wealth of the Buddha's teachings through the analysis and treatises of T'ien-t'ai and the importance of the concept of ichinen sanzen. Saicho, later renamed Dengyo is recognized as the founder of the Tendai school of Buddhsim in Japan. He founded the temple and headquarters of Tendai at Enryakuji on Mt. Hiei near Kyoto. He is also said to have been the first to bring tea to Japan. After his death, he was awarded the posthumous title of Dengyō Daishi (伝教大師).

Gongyo and the Daimoku

As one studies what has been historically referred to as the 80 or 84 thousand teachings of the Buddha it becomes apparent that the "practice" or daily ritual of Buddhism has been widely interpreted, widely debated, and fundamentally regionalized in many cases. So what is the "correct" practice of the Buddhist teachings?

It can easily be argued and shown that the advent of the monk Nichiren and his lifetime of teaching and reformation of Buddhism was specifically to answer this question. In fact, Nichiren answered this question so definitively that he was able to prove that to practice in any other way was strictly against the Buddha's own teachings and therefore not Buddhism at all, but some egotistic and defiled insult to the Buddha himself. This may sound an arrogant statement, but the extreme degree of scholarship Nichiren developed and used in conjunction with the respect and citations he culled from previous amazing scholars from Miao-lo, Dengyo, T'ien-t'ai, to Vasubandhu, Nagarjuna, and the Buddha's own words, leave little doubt that his elucidations, teachings, and admonitions, all deserve the highest merit. Nichiren created nothing new. He simply made obvious what was already evident in the scholarship and the texts of the Buddha's teachings, but previously obfuscated by tradition, and lack of capacity to understand.

Nichiren returned many times in his writings to T'ien-t'ai's codification of the Buddha's teachings. A tremendous amount of analysis and scholarship supported the supreme import of the final two teachings of the Buddha. The Lotus Sutra (Teaching of the Magnificent Lotus Flower) and the Mahaparinirvana Sutra often called simply the Nirvana Sutra. Of these the Nirvana Sutra is the teaching Buddha spoke on his deathbed awaiting Nirvana, in which he references his ultimate teaching as the Lotus Sutra. In fact, it is in the Lotus Sutra that the Buddha clearly states that all Sutras, or teachings, he had taught previous to the Lotus Sutra did not contain the ultimate truth. The truth, he would now reveal in this Lotus Sutra, the ultimate law, teaching, and method of all Buddhas throughout all time for the direct attainment of enlightenment. It could not be clearer. Any school of Buddhism devoted to any previous sutra or group of sutras was no longer practicing the Buddha's teaching, but instead something inferior that did not achieve the Buddha's stated goal of enlightenment for all, and therefore not Buddhism. This is a strict statement, but totally valid in the context of the Buddha's lifetime of teaching, allowing for no error of interpretation or deviation. The Buddha's teachings are always repeated in varied rhetoric and repeatedly with extreme minutia in order to prevent any deviation or misinterpretation. So it follows that when the Buddha says everything I taught you before did not contain the truth, so get ride of it, and now listen to me carefully as I tell you the absolute and ultimate truth, we should do exactly as he says. Additionally, in the Lotus Sutra, the Buddha explains why it had to be this way, as he uses the story of a father with three sons who get sick upon the father's travels away from home. When the father returns and finds his sons sick, he immediately makes a medicine for them to take. However, only one of his sons takes the medicine and gets well, while the others, too deluded by sickness to trust their father, refuse to take the medicine and continue to be sick. The father, fearing the death of his two remaining sons tells his sons he must again leave the home and travel afar. Once the father is away from home, he sends back word by messenger that he has perished in an accident. Upon receiving the word of their dead father, the two sick sons take the medicine believing there is no longer any reason for them to live, and they get well. Now that all sons are recovering and lamenting the death of their father, the father returns to greet his sons and celebrate their good health.

With this story the Buddha illustrates that while one might consider the father a liar for deceiving his sick sons, it is more true that the father's actions were built of compassion in order to subvert the sons' delusions and to help them in taking the medicine they so desperately needed. It is this example the Buddha uses to justify his holding back of the ultimate and true teaching of the ultimate law or practice for immediate enlightenment. Again, it is quite clear that the Lotus Sutra is to be regarded as the one true teaching for the attainment of Buddhahood.

This is so obvious to Nichiren that he cannot hold back his ire at the many schools of Buddhism enjoying favor in his day that practice mystical or terribly misguided rituals and calling themselves Buddhists. From chanting certain Buddhas' names to arduous mental exercises and myriad meditation techniques all derived by people and not substantiated in the Buddha's own teachings. For instance, the practice by so many sects of "Buddhism" to chant at the base of large statues of some Buddha is a practice specifically forbidden by the Buddha's teaching. And this makes complete sense. For if you understand that Buddha is not a person, but a state of Being, which is non-substantial (un-differentiated, non-dimensional, quiescent), then the idea of praying to a statue is complete attachment to this Samsaric illusionary realm and misleads away from enlightenment rather than toward it!

So the burden of making explicit the correct way to practice the teachings of the Buddha, Nichiren fully appreciates and makes his life's work. First he realizes through all his travels from temple to honored residence wherever sacred Buddhist texts are stored and the immense library of teachings, treatises, and explanations of treatises that he has studied since the age of twelve, make the following points abundantly evident as the true teachings of the Buddha:

❏ The Lotus Sutra is the "king" of all teachings

❏ The title of the Lotus Sutra contains all of the Buddha's lifetime of teachings, and is in fact invoked at the beginning of each of the twenty-eight chapters of the Lotus Sutra

- Of the first fourteen chapters, the second chapter contains the pragmatic teaching of the Sutra, and the sixteenth chapter of the later fourteen chapters contains the core of the essential teachings of the Buddha

From this Nichiren arrives at the single practice the Buddha revealed that would enable anybody to attain immediate awakening and guarantee eventual Buddhahood in this lifetime. Chanting is a form of active meditation that has been around since time immemorial. Silent meditation is mainly passive and can be directed with the mind, but is very difficult to master and requires a monk's existence in seclusion to do so. So, secluded meditation, or silent meditation, although helpful as a part of training, can never be considered a universal way for anybody to attain enlightenment. Chanting, however, involves a conviction of performing an action not only on thought, and in deed, but also in speech. Speech is a very powerful cause maker. So to combine all three of our human cause makers into one action are not only very powerful but also very universal. To add even more power to this formula, it is excruciatingly obvious how distracted and unstable the human mind can be unless it has a physical object to focus attention upon. But as the Buddha taught, images of the Buddha or statues were antithetical to correct practice. At once the answer presented itself. It was the title of the ultimate sutra that was the obvious tool! By chanting the title of the Sutra, "Myohorengekyo" preceded by a declaration of one's conviction and determined goal of enlightenment, "Namu", one could accomplish the most powerful meditation. But to maintain focus and supercharge that practice to train the mind against distraction and to cement the will toward awakening and maintaining one's innate Buddha nature, would require a simple scroll with the characters of the title of the sutra and the dedication at the top for an object to secure focused meditation. Understand that the scroll, now called a Gohonzon, is not worshiped, but instead represents as a physical avatar, the Buddha-nature and all of the Buddha's teachings already inherent within life. To quote from Nichiren:

> "...no treasure tower exists other than the figures of the men and women who embrace the Lotus Sutra. It follows, therefore, that whether eminent or humble, high or low, those who chant Namu-Myohorengekyo, are themselves the treasure tower, and, likewise, are themselves the Thus Come One Many Treasures. No treasure tower exists other than Myoho-Renge-Kyo. The Daimoku of the Lotus Sutra is the treasure tower, and the treasure tower is Namu-Myohorengekyo."

From the Major Writings of Nichiren. *"On the Treasure Tower"*.

And also from "The Real Aspect of the Gohonzon":

> Never seek this Gohonzon outside yourself. The Gohonzon exists only within the mortal flesh of us ordinary people who embrace the Lotus Sutra and chant Namu-Myohorengekyo. The body is the palace of the ninth consciousness, the unchanging reality that reigns over all of life's functions. To be endowed

with the Ten Worlds means that all ten, without a single exception, exist in one world. Because of this it is called a mandala. Mandala is a Sanskrit word that is translated as "perfectly endowed" or "a cluster of blessings." This Gohonzon also is found only in the two characters for conviction and a strong mind. This is what the sutra means when it states that one can "gain entrance through conviction and a strong mind alone."

So here is established the essential practice of True Buddhism. And just to make the point ever so clear, please indulge me in two more quotations from Nichiren's major writings:

From "The One Essential Phrase":

"... By this he means that, although for the sake of brevity only the title of the sutra is spoken, the entire sutra is contained in the title alone.

Everything has its essential point, and the heart of the Lotus Sutra is its title, or the Daimoku, of Namu-Myohorengekyo. Truly, if you chant this in the morning and evening, you are correctly reading the entire Lotus Sutra. Chanting Daimoku twice is the same as reading the entire sutra twice, one hundred Daimoku equal one hundred readings of the sutra, and one thousand Daimoku, one thousand readings of the sutra. Thus, if you ceaselessly chant Daimoku, you will be continually reading the Lotus Sutra. The sixty volumes of the T'ien-t'ai doctrines give exactly the same interpretation. A teaching this easy to uphold and this easy to practice was expounded for the sake of all living beings in the evil world of this latter age."

From "The Daimoku of the Lotus Sutra":

"To accept, uphold, read, recite, take delight in, and protect all the eight volumes and twenty-eight chapters of the Lotus Sutra is called the comprehensive practice. To accept, uphold, and protect the "Expedient Means" chapter and the "Life Span" chapter is called the abbreviated practice. And simply to chant one four-phrase verse or the Daimoku, and to protect those who do so, is called the essential practice. Hence, among these three kinds of practice, comprehensive, abbreviated, and essential, the Daimoku is defined as the essential practice."

Now as you can see there is talk of different levels of practice here. And this is where we introduce Gongyo. As the Buddha taught that the attainment or awakening of our Buddha-nature could be achieved with conviction alone, that conviction comes as the result of daily effort, and consistent study. The simplest study comes from the recitation of the two standout chapters of the Lotus Sutra. And so a form of repeated recitation and five distinct meditations at the end of the recitations supply a strong structure and easily practiced consistent study habit. Together these elements constitute the Liturgy of True Buddhism.

Although Quantum Life Buddhism may be viewed as a Nichiren school of Buddhism, we must be clear here. There are a few schools of Nichiren Buddhism. The one thing they all have in common is their adherence to Nichiren's writings and some sort of claim to lineage directly from Nichiren through one or another disciple or land owner. Need I state again that we are practicing Buddhism, the teachings of the Buddha? Although we respect with great reverence the contributions of Nichiren, let us not forget that the greatness and loftiness of his contribution exists only as it stands on the shoulders of Saicho, Miao-lo, the amazing scholarship of T'ien-t'ai, Vasubandhu, Nagarjuna, and ultimately, the Buddha's every word. Quantum Life Buddhism is the study, practice, and conviction of the teachings of Buddha. We pay homage and great respect to all those scholars who dedicated their lives to the correct transmission of the Buddha's teachings, and we use the tremendous knowledge they provide us. We also know from the true teachings, that the wisdom to be gained from this knowledge is something that we must gain for ourselves through the very methods taught by the Buddha and elucidated through these sages.

Study inherent in five meditations of Gongyo

First meditation

In the first meditation we focus our thoughts of gratitude to the Shoten Zenjin. The names of the Shoten Zenjin listed are derived from the history of Buddhism throughout many Asian cultures. The strengths and special characteristics of each of them are strictly symbolic. The deeper meaning of this meditation is to acknowledge the presence of our essential Buddha-nature functioning within our lives. Those moments when we cannot explain our sudden acumen or our extreme good fortune in the face of tremendous peril or challenge. We have all had those moments when either as it happened or in retrospect we cannot fathom the powers that kept us from grievous harm or tremendous embarrassment, or even when we succeeded so well at some endeavor that we feel we were especially endowed for just that moment. These are the forces from deep within our lives that we have brought with us into our journey of Samsara and which will follow us back into the quiescence of eternity.

Second meditation

The second meditation expresses our appreciation for the teachings of the Buddha. We start with the fundamental and essential law of self-manifestation that is the core of all the Buddha's teaching and expressed as

Myohorengekyo. This truth is explained within the second (Juryo) chapter of the Lotus Sutra and is praised as contained within the supreme teachings of the Lotus Sutra. Further appreciation is extended to the fabric of this essential expression of truth in acknowledgement that it is the very essence of the universe, the perfect fusion of Taiji and Qi as we discussed earlier. In this meditation we first praise the law of Myohorengekyo, and then follow it through its manifestations and process to Samsara, from the entity of time without beginning (our quiescent state), the Buddha of absolute freedom (free from all attachments and desires), the eternal manifestation of the Ten Worlds (aggregates), the embodiment of Ichinen Sanzen (tendencies and conditions), the oneness of person and law (as we are our own creators), and finally the manifestation of all phenomena as both a reflection and a result of our own making in this universe, impermanent and having no self-nature. The last portion stating our thanks for the immeasurable benefits we have received, because we now understand the precious beauty of our manifestation and the opportunity we now have to perceive this grand eternal existence we truly have.

Third meditation

In the third meditation we offer our appreciation to all those sages who dedicated their lives to the correct transmission of the Buddha's teaching. We especially honor those of great import to our current depth of understanding including Nichiren, T'ien-t'ai, Dengyo, Miao-lo, Vasubandhu, and Nagarjuna. Then we offer appreciation to all teachings that in their ultimate use will lead us to more and more teachings and eventually to the discovery of the Buddhist teachings. Since we are the entire same essential core, it follows that no matter how diverse, all teachings are ultimately Buddhist.

Fourth meditation

The fourth meditation turns inward and begins with a sincere concentration on the Buddhist teachings to touch all human beings to accomplish a balance of Buddhist practitioners, Buddhist sympathizers, and as well as those who know but are not interested, inclined, or even un-accepting of Buddhist. The goal in this is to achieve a balance of influences so as to have the strength of human character throughout the world to end and stop conflict resolution through war, and to bring about a more peaceful existence here. In this goal we focus again our thoughts, but this time on the erasure of our own negative aggregates of tendencies and conditions to clear up our own behaviors and to reveal our true Buddha-nature, and to maintain it in this lifetime, now and throughout eternity.

Fifth meditation

And finally in the last meditation we reach beyond ourselves back to the origins and to the future. Here we offer our thoughts and energy to those who have passed away in our families, our ancestry and all those around us. We offer our thoughts as we ring a bell, hoping to carry our thoughts on the vibrations of the bell tones into the deep space of those passed but still present through our Buddha-nature connection. After offering our silent thoughts we then focus on the spread of the Buddha's teachings contained in the threefold lotus sutra throughout the world to bring happiness and peace to mankind via the true teaching of Buddhism.

Quantum Life Buddhism

Deep Understanding, Deep Practice, Awakening

We have a tremendous advantage over the people of ancient times today in the absolute surfeit of information. But, information is useless without understanding that leads to the organization of such information. This is knowledge, and yet knowledge is also of little use lest we understand more deeply how this knowledge is to be applied. Once we understand the application of knowledge culled from information, only then can we begin to function in some constructive manner, and yet even then we are confounded with obstacles and unexpected results. Finally we gain wisdom, from repeated failure and disappointment, we may or may not realize success, but we most certainly arrive at greater wisdom. So how can we arrive at this greater wisdom without the years of obstacles, failures, and disappointments! That is truly the question of all time. It might be said of this query that it is in fact the modern equivalent of enlightenment.

The Buddha taught that the only path to wisdom is to study, and that study must be motivated by conviction and consistent (practice). This is true in life, Samsara, and the attainment of ultimate wisdom, the wisdom of Buddhahood.

Body, Mind, Essential Creative Core

Let us return to the visualization of the flattened city with all its myriad physical and emotional attributes, its predilections and desires, all of the life-conditions and realms of existence. When we visualized this absolutely crushed plane to the degree that it became a non-dimensional mathematical abstraction, we still retained in it the "essence" of all potentials that we began the process with. So, like the old spaghetti sauce commercial, if we sought to find potential for any of the 100 life-conditions, or the 3 realms of existence, or the 10 factors of life, well, "It's in there". It simply exists in a state of quiescence. To help understand what this means I would like to use an example from our physical world that has already been scientifically proven and is in use today.

You may be familiar today with the term "stem-cell". Stem cell research has been at the forefront of many discussions and debate for some twenty years now. Mind you this analogy is limited to our physical world, but I think it may illustrate the truth of the state of Buddhahood versus the state of Samsara rather nicely.

The stem cell is the simplest cell within an organism. Specifically, we will use in this analogy, the human stem cell. There are hundreds of millions of cells within the human body all doing one specific task in concert with the other cells. Skin cells replenish and rebuild our flesh constantly, while just slightly different cells replenish the sub-layers of flesh, and other tissues necessary for our bodies to function. Liver cells, brain cells, lung cells, and cells that provide fluids all are constantly being replenished from the source in our bodies of all cells, our bone marrow. It is nearly magical how the cells that comprise our entire body and organs and fluids constantly regenerate from our marrow. Even more brilliant is that the marrow is not simply a storehouse of specific kinds of cells, acting like a distribution warehouse and pulling this or that kind of cell as needed. Our bone marrow is much more efficient than that. Instead, the bone marrow manufactures one cell with the "potential" to be any cell the body needs. In fact, these cells, stem cells, are so generic, that they can be moved from person to person with absolutely no differentiation. Perhaps you can begin to understand or appreciate the medical and scientific excitement about stem cells.

When cells are called for, from anywhere in our bodies, stem cells (essence) are sent through the marrow, combined with specific genetic information derived from our DNA (tendencies and conditions) and "become" (aggregate) specific cells on their way to the requisite tissue, organ, or fluid (birth). In parenthesis are my analogous notes in reference to the conditioned genesis or 12 Nidanna discussed earlier.

So in this analogy, the quiescent state of Buddhahood is likened to bone-marrow, where all potential exists and when motivated by desire, combines essence, with tendencies and conditions to produce viable entities to combine or birth into the fabric of sentient and insentient beings in Samsara. I am careful to state both sentient and insentient beings here because it is important to understand that at the "stem-cell" or quiescent potential level, human birth is no different from trees, rocks, or antelope birth. The only thing that differentiates us is tendencies and conditions, the aggregates. Perhaps this will also help you to understand the meaning of the word often heard but rarely defined, "oneness" with all "things".

Since all "things" are created from this state of quiescence or Buddhahood, I find it easier to translate its reality or truth in pragmatic terms for use here in Samsara. The Buddha used the term for this as he was simply there, and teaching being there. However, I find that the term Buddha has accrued so much charisma and misinterpretation over the centuries that a different term is needed to differentiate the truth, from the history. So, in Quantum Life Buddhism, this pool of ultimate wisdom is termed the "Essential Creative Core".

I believe this is a much stronger and satisfying term than all previous attempts at labeling this truth as it allows access to it for all of us. Perhaps it is because we have finally developed the capacity for this wisdom. Perhaps it is as the Buddha's prediction that this wisdom, this state of Buddha 2500 years after his Nirväna, should now enable the spread of True Buddhism, True Wisdom, True Insight, throughout the world. Previous terms like spirit, or gods of all manner, astral planes and "higher" powers, all are so completely vague and ill defined if at all. They represent a lack of wisdom, a fondling of knowledge without understanding. The Essential Creative Core answers directly the question, "Where do we come from", clearly defined and scientifically proven. And by reversal of the process, it is also simple to answer, "Where do we go".

As Nagarjuna reiterated the Buddha's true teaching, in as far as our Buddha-nature we neither come nor go, neither exists nor not exists. There is no Atman nor Anatman, no soul or non-soul; there is no vessel of each of us individually anywhere. Buddhahood, which is our true entity, simply "is", eternally as our "essential creative core". It is only in Samsara that we perceive ourselves as small parts of that entity, each of us representing a function within the whole. Those distinctions we give ourselves to demand that we are unique, are the product of aggregate groups of subtle and strong tendencies and conditions we amassed on our way to this instantiation of the potential for life. Once we realize that at our Core, there is absolutely no difference in anything, that is when we begin to gain the Buddha wisdom and quell our reactionary mind, quiet our tendencies, travel through this life in greater peace, appreciation, and an appropriate awe for all that is creation. Only then, after much study, observation, and practice can we deepen our conviction, our knowledge, and our wisdom that we are the entire creator, of our own creation and all that surrounds us.

Quantum Life Buddhism helps to evolve this wisdom through the study of all the Buddhist texts as well as a focus on the Arts in both their Visual/Aural aspects and their Martial aspects.

The Fine Arts help us to "see" the world without the obstacles of rules, rhetoric, or cultural restriction. The language of the Arts also helps us more quickly convert information into wisdom with little pause for categorical knowledge. Once again we mirror the true teachings in that there is no separation from our enlightenment in this form. Samsara, though it is a creation or construct of our own making, it is as much our enlightenment as quiescence. All that is needed is to shed the illusions of our aggregates to appreciate fully the life eternal. The Fine Arts are a bridge to that understanding.

Martial Arts allow us to generate health for our bodies, to strengthen and sharpen our physical as well as our mental skills. This training is critical in the exercise of training the mind, to teach us focus, concentration, and self-control. With discipline, again we mirror the Buddha's teaching for consistent study and firm conviction, as we develop strong minds capable of deep focus, discernment, and abstraction.

The Essential Creative Core is ultimately better attained and more solidly understood when the studies of Buddha's teachings are conjoined with mental acuity and freedom of abstraction developed through the Arts. It can be shown over the centuries that the ultimate goal of all Arts has been and remains a transcendence of mortal follies and delusion. It was the Buddha's wish from the start and with every word spoken that all should attain enlightenment and that the path would be available to any, no matter what status or station.

Through the Quantum Life Buddhist practice of Chanting meditation, Qigong meditation and health exercises, Study resources, and Training in the Arts, we offer a life path of support and access to health, happiness, and wisdom for anyone.

Appendix

Citta

Citta (Pali) is one of three overlapping terms used in the Nikäyas to refer to the mind, the others being **Manas** and **Viññana**. Each is sometimes used in the generic and non-technical sense of "mind" in general, and the three are sometimes used in sequence to refer to one's mental processes as a whole. Their primary uses are, however, distinct.

"Citta" primarily represents one's mindset, or state of mind. Citta is the term used in to refer to the quality of mental processes as a whole. Citta is neither an entity nor a process; and these likely account for its not being classified as a khanda, nor mentioned in the paticcasamuppada formula.

The complex causal nexus of volitions (or intentions) which one experiences continuously conditions one's thoughts, speech, and actions. One's state of mind at any given time reflects that complex; thus, the causal origin of actions, speech, and thoughts is sometimes associated with the state of mind (citta), in a manner of speaking. This does not mean that it is that causal nexus; it is better understood as an abstract reflection. One's mind-set can be out of tune with one's desires or aspirations. In that it reflects the volitions, the citta is said to go off with a will of its own if not properly controlled. It may lead a person astray or, if properly controlled, directed, and integrated, ennoble one. One may "make citta turn according to" his wishes most effectively by developing skill in meditative concentration which brings mental calm and clarity. An individual undergoes many different states of mind; The **Majjhima Nikaya**.II.27 asks: "Which citta? Fore citta is manifold, various, and diverse." Generally speaking, a person will operate with a collection of changing mindsets, and some will occur regularly. While these mindsets determine the personality, they are not in control of themselves, but fluctuate and alternate. There is thus the need for the meditative integration of personality to provide a greater, more wholesome consistency.

Regarding volitions, there is a similarity between Viññana and citta; they are both associated with the qualitative condition of a human being. Viññana provides awareness and continuity by which one knows one's moral condition, and citta is an abstraction representing that condition. Citta is therefore closely related to volitions; this connection is also etymological, as citta comes from the same verbal root in Pali as the active terms meaning, "To will." Citta also reflects one's cognitive condition/progress.

Citta as a mindset can become "contracted" (i.e., unworkable), "distracted", "grown great", "composed", or the opposite of such qualities. It can be dominated by a certain emotion, so as to be "terrified", "astonished", or "tranquil." It can be "taken hold of" by pleasant or unpleasant impressions. A host of negative emotionally charged states can pertain to it, or it may be free of such states, so it is vital to develop or purify it: "For a long time this citta has been defiled by attachment, hatred, and delusion. By defilement of citta, beings are defiled; by purity of citta, beings are purified".

In the Anguttara Nikàya, it is stated; "The citta is luminous, but it is defiled by defilements from outside." This does not suggest an "original purity"; as one's state of mind is an abstraction, there is an abstract sense in which one's citta could be thought of in principle as pure. Just as a pool of water might be thought in principle to have a calm surface, which displays ripples and muddiness, so one's state of mind might be thought to in principle be luminous (as in Janna) but to display all mental activity.

Attaining a purified citta corresponds to the attaining of liberating insight. This indicates that a liberated one's state of mind reflects no ignorance or defilements. As these represent bondage, their absence is described in terms of freedom.

The Ten Worlds

One of the main concepts of Buddhism, and one that is crucial to understanding Buddhist method is the concept of life condition. If you don't understand the concept of life condition, it's going to be very hard to understand what an enlightened life condition is; and that, after all, is what the practice of Buddhism is all about.

Basic to the concept of life condition is a Buddhist term known as the Ten Worlds. The Ten Worlds are not physical places. They are momentary states or conditions of life that each person can experience at any given time. These conditions by themselves, in combinations, and always shifting, are the lens through which our behaviors and actions are shaped and influenced even before our conscious mind gets hold. When we refer to the concept of "life condition," we are referring to the Ten Worlds. The first six are most common in which people live all of the time. They are commonly known as the "six lower worlds." Each of us has a "central aggregate tendency" associated with some combination of them. That is, there is a particular life condition that you will always go back to whenever there is a lack of internal or external stimuli to activate a different one. So then, to describe them, they are:

Hell (Jap. Jigoku).

This state of life is characterized by a feeling of hopelessness; sadness, depression, lack of confidence, tiredness, and the sense that nothing will change for the better and that there is nothing anyone can do to change it. This state can manifest as uncontrollable rage, not to be confused with anger, but a desperate and deep self-hatred.

Hunger or Hungry Ghosts (Jap. Gaki).

This is a feeling of insatiable desire. It could be a desire for food, but usually denotes a "need" for some external stimulus the person in this world thinks will result in their happiness. Examples of things a person might hunger for are cars, houses, money, drugs, alcohol, someone, etc. The moment you are in the world of hunger, you are, a slave to your desires.

Animality or Animals (Jap. Chikusho).

A person in this world behaves like an animal in that they prey on those whom they perceive to be weaker than them and cower before those whom they perceive to be more powerful than them. Work environments are perhaps the most common places where behaviors arising from this world occur. A person in this world may pretend to willingly do everything that their boss tells them and to respect their boss's authority while treating their own subordinates in a high-handed or authoritarian manner. Another description of Animality is contained in the common phrase "the law of the jungle." The struggle for power becomes all consuming and fear of others with more power than you debilitate you for the moment when you are in this world or life condition.

Anger or Asuras (Jap. Shura).

The world of anger is perhaps the most deceptively named of the Ten Worlds. It is a condition of egotism and self-righteousness, backstabbing and manipulation. Like Animality, it is a condition that is focused on power. Wars start from the collective life condition of a nation centered in the world of anger. The concept that was once popular in our country propounded, "We are America. We are the best country in the world. We must fight to make the world safe for democracy so that all others can be just like us." Dogmatism about religion, politics, relationships, etc. comes from this life condition. All others are to believe you because of who you are (your status and previous accomplishments) not because what you are saying is necessarily reasonable or correct.

These four lower worlds, or life conditions, are known as the four evil paths. That is because they tend to lead individuals down to the lowest condition — the world of hell. Those in the world of hunger, for example, after they have exhausted all efforts to obtain what they desire and cannot do so, quickly plunge into the condition of hell or hopelessness. This is especially true if they believe that their desire is the only means of attaining happiness for themselves. As for the condition of Animality, you also begin to feel helpless and hopeless unless you have found a way to become the "top dog" in the most important aspects of your daily life. Then you become entrenched in the world of anger, thinking yourself superior to all others and forcing your will on everyone around you. At that point, those with more power will meet your unrelenting, yet egotistical attitude. Or you may be faced by those who can clearly point out your errors and cause others, from whom you obtained your power of anger in the first place, to lose respect and quit following you. Rich people who flaunt their wealth, such as newly rich athletes, begin to feel so powerful that they actually become outraged when some authorities point out that they cannot break the laws about use of drugs or other things no matter who they think they are.

Humanity or Human Beings (also called Tranquility, Jap. Nin).

This is another world that is somewhat difficult to describe. This state is often mistaken for enlightenment (research Ch'an or Zen) even by Buddhists. This is a life condition of stasis, where the perception is that nothing changes. It is a condition where you can use rational judgment. You can carry on conversations and have dialogues without becoming distraught about concerns for your own life or the lives of others. This condition is actually the goal of many people. This is what they strive for. They believe that if they could just become tranquil, then they wouldn't need anything else in their lives. One of the problems with this world is that while in it, you really can't accomplish much of anything at all. Desire causes people to take action, sometimes for good and sometimes for bad. When people are in the world of humanity, they are absent from desire. This can be a good thing, and usually feels good to the person experiencing it. However, desire goes beyond selfishness sometimes and extends to helping others. For instance, one might feel a desire to stop animal abuse. In the world of tranquility however, such a desire would be absent. So it becomes difficult to get much accomplished while in this state, either for oneself or for others. So much effort is put forth to avoid emotionalism or passion that, despite what you would think at first view, this world is actually exhausting in that it is impossible to remain in without just shutting out the realities of your life and the lives of others.

Rapture or Heavenly Beings (Jap. Ten).

The condition of rapture, as the name implies, is one of elation or ecstasy. It can be the result of a positive outcome within the world of hunger. Obtaining what you wanted brings about a feeling of elation that consumes you for the moment. A main characteristic of this condition is that it is short lived.

Most people tend to cycle through these six lower worlds over and over again without any hope of breaking free from them. For instance, a person may hunger for a certain job; say to be a rock star. They devote their lives to the goal (Namu) for several years. When they reach their goal, assuming that they have the fortune to do so, they at first live in the world of rapture. They may then lose their stardom or become tired of it and the lack of privacy. They will then fall into the world of hell or back into hunger for some other circumstance they think will bring them happiness. Another example would be of yearning for a new car. After working hard to get the car and living in the world of hunger, the person will switch to the world of rapture once they achieve their goal. After a while, the good feelings about having a new car fade. The person may then enter tranquility or even hunger again. That is the constant cycle of the six lower worlds. Their environment easily manipulates the person, and their happiness relies heavily upon their external success.

The preceding examples are cases of people with pretty good fortune or who have made reasonably good causes in their present or previous lives. A person who has made bad causes may have a very difficult time ever escaping from hell or hunger. Such a person will make further bad causes by committing crimes or perhaps even suicide. We see such examples every day. That leads to the next concept of the Ten Worlds. As we had mentioned earlier, most people stay around a single world most of the time. The world that a person hovers around is known as their central life tendency. The central life tendency of most humans is tranquility (a.k.a. humanity). The important thing to understand about the concept of the Ten Worlds and life condition is that it is relatively easy to obtain external goals, but to change one's central life tendency is quite difficult. Even after obtaining a new car, a person will shortly fall from the world of rapture into their old feeling or life tendency. So, to be able to maintain a high life condition, or central life tendency, is the most fortunate thing a person could have. To raise one's life condition, or central life tendency, is also the most difficult thing a person can do. Many people think that the fifth and sixth worlds (tranquility and rapture) are the happiest states of life that anyone can achieve. They strive to maintain one of these two worlds as much as they possibly can. The fortunate ones are capable of staying in one of those two worlds most of the time. Some people, on the other hand, realize that there must be more to life and strive for an even higher state of life, or life condition. That leads us to the next worlds.

Learning or Voice Hearers (Jap. Shomon).

As the name of this world implies, the world of learning is exhibited when you are gaining knowledge about the world around you or your life itself. To begin to learn, that is to be in the world of learning, you must exert effort. It is said that a seeking mind is the key to wisdom, and you've probably heard teachers say that without effort on the part of their students, learning will not take place. Put another way, your external environment cannot make you learn. It can provide great circumstances to learn, but it cannot make you learn or be in the world of learning.

Realization or Cause-Awakened Ones (Jap. Engaku).

The world of realization takes learning one step further. It requires even more effort. Perhaps the easiest way to describe what takes place within the world of realization is to look to the arts. Just because you know the notes that a guitar can make doesn't make you a great musician. Similarly, your learning and knowledge about painting does not make you a great artist. By internalizing the knowledge and adding something of yourself and your creativity to it, you can take your learning a step further and actually go beyond the level of your teachers.

While these two worlds, learning and realization are much "higher" life conditions and allow you much more control than the six lower worlds; they still have their shortcomings. First of all, to remain for long in these worlds you must be somewhat self-absorbed. It is a limited sort of enlightenment that excludes most others. It most frequently leads to the world of anger where the person can't understand why others can't just do things as well as they do them. They grow impatient with the entire world around them. They think themselves somehow superior because of their knowledge and the efforts that they had to put out to get themselves where they are now. They have little time or patience for others who won't or can't do what they did. People in these worlds don't care to waste their time convincing others to follow their example. They believe that teaching others won't help them further their knowledge or the realization of their art and self-expression anyway, so why bother.

Bodhisattva (Jap. Bodhisattva).

The world of Bodhisattva is a naturally occurring condition of life, although most people don't think it is. Most people think that the term Bodhisattva applies only to Buddhists, but that is not true. It is the life condition where you actually care about another person's life more than you do your own. Say, for instance, that there is someone in the world who is trapped in a burning building. To make a decision to risk your own life to save another's is the condition of Bodhisattva. At the moment you decided to do so, you are in the world of Bodhisattva. You may not stay there very long, but it is an extremely powerful good cause to make for your life. Because it is so hard to love, to care, even beyond your own self-protection and preservation, it is a life condition that also yields a great cause and effect within your life. If you were to constantly find yourself in situations that gave you the opportunity to offer your life for the sake of others, and if you constantly gave no thought to yourself or your own self preservation, but freely gave of yourself, you would be accomplishing an extremely difficult feat and would be making an extremely good cause. But actually, in real life, even those people such as emergency workers who have chosen to put their lives in situations where they themselves may die trying to save others, exhibit the life condition of tranquility, anger, or Animality about the career choice they have made. They do not consistently act out of Bodhisattva compassion where it is the love and concern they feel for the person, which instigates their every action. Actually, the only way to consistently experience the world of Bodhisattva is by raising your life condition to the next and highest world — the world of Buddhahood. The world of Bodhisattva actually enhances and strengthens the world of Buddhahood. In other words, they act reciprocally to enhance each other.

To quote Shakyamuni Buddha about this "…Originally I practiced the Bodhisattva way, and the life span that I acquired then has yet to come to an end but will last twice the number of years that have already passed." (Lotus Sutra) Both the story of heroic Bodhisattva deeds, and the deeds themselves, lives on and on. The world of Bodhisattva strengthens, or you might say lengthens, the condition of Buddhahood.

Buddhahood or Buddha (Jap. Butsu).

This world, or life condition, is the most difficult to explain. It is the condition of life that exhibits infinite wisdom, strong life force and vitality, and tremendous good fortune. Buddha wisdom here does not refer to knowledge. Everyone has inherent wisdom. When you are in the right place at the right time and do the right thing for your life and when your life just kind of "knows" what to do, we say that you are in the world of Buddhahood. When you chant Namu-Myoho-Renge-Kyo, you are instantaneously in the world of Buddhahood. Your conscious mind may not know it at the time, but you are actually there. You exhibit what is known as absolute happiness. Your life condition is not dependent on your environment at that moment. For the moment, you have secured for yourself a condition of pure joy, comfort and freedom, even in the most unlikely of circumstances. Even in circumstances that others would think that you couldn't help but be suffering, the enlightened life condition of Buddhahood won't let you suffer. It's really strange to experience, but quite real and quite wondrous. To quote the teachings of Shakyamuni again, "...This, my land, remains safe and tranquil.... The halls and pavilions in its gardens and groves are adorned with various kinds of gems. Jeweled trees abound in flowers and fruit where living beings enjoy themselves at ease.... My pure land is not destroyed, yet the multitude sees it as consumed in fire, with anxiety, fear and other sufferings filling it everywhere." (Lotus Sutra) Here, Shakyamuni is

- 105 -

referring to the condition of Buddhahood rather than a specific place. He is commenting on the wondrous nature of the condition of enlightenment, as it exists in the real world. The goal in Buddhism is to make enlightenment one's central life tendency. We mentioned before that a person's ability to make a certain world their central life tendency is the result of causes that they have made in the past. Some people spend their entire lives striving to break free from a central life tendency of hell. For one to raise their central life tendency at all takes tremendous effort, struggle, wisdom and good fortune. Therefore, for a person to raise their central life tendency to that of enlightenment is an incredible struggle. It is not something that a person can accomplish by simply trying to do it, or even by reading about how to do it. A person needs help in breaking free from the negative causes they have made in the past that keep them trapped in the world, or life condition, in which they presently live. They need something powerful enough to counteract all of the past bad causes that they have made. There is only one cause that is powerful enough to overturn any past negative cause and permanently raise a person's central life tendency. That cause is to chant Namu-Myoho-Renge-Kyo and teach it to others.

Within each of the Ten Worlds is the potential for each of the other nine. This is referred to as the mutual possession of the Ten Worlds. What this means in practical terms is that the potential for Buddhahood exists within each of the other worlds. You don't have to scratch and claw your way up through each and every one of the worlds to reach the highest or tenth world of

Buddhahood. As you become aware of your life's tendency to cycle among the lower six worlds, you can develop a seeking mind to escape from them. Your efforts even to read this book about Buddhism are the cause for you to break free from the six lower worlds' grasp. When you take the initiative to have a seeking mind, you ask questions and are in the world of learning. As you internalize this information about Buddhism, you may be in the world of realization, or you may even seek out the means to end suffering for the sake of another and be in the world of Bodhisattva.

If you chant Namu-Myoho-Renge-Kyo as you study this text, you will find yourself in the enlightened world (or Buddhahood) of learning, realization, or Bodhisattva, by virtue of the mutual possession of the Ten Worlds and the power of chanting Namu-Myoho-Renge-Kyo. Even if your karma has it that your central life tendency is that of hell, as you chant Namu-Myoho-Renge-Kyo, you will easily and quickly escape the sufferings of hell and find yourself with a renewed hope for your own and others' future. If you fail to chant Namu-Myoho-Renge-Kyo, though, you can never understand or experience the world of Buddhahood in your own life. Chanting Namu-Myoho-Renge-Kyo is not about Buddha wisdom, it is Buddha wisdom. As Shakyamuni Buddha said, "The true entity of all phenomena can only be understood and shared between Buddha's." (Lotus Sutra) Therefore, the only way to do more than intellectualize the concept of the world of Buddhahood is to start chanting Namu-Myoho-Renge-Kyo now and reveal the condition of Buddhahood within. The accomplishment of enlightenment, or in other words, making the world of

Buddhahood your life's central tendency requires Buddhist practice. As we have stated before, the moment you chant Namu-Myoho-Renge-Kyo, your life is in the world of Buddhahood. The moment you stop, your life returns to one of the other nine worlds, which is a process dependent upon your karma. Here an analogy may help you to understand the process of enlightenment. Suppose your life is a piece of steel and chanting Namu- Myoho-Renge-Kyo is like a magnet. The instant the steel (your life) touches the magnet (your chanting) it takes on magnetic properties. While actually physically in contact with the magnet, the steel itself is magnetized. When you release the steel from the magnet, the steel's magnetic properties go away. But repeatedly rubbing the steel against the magnet causes the steel to retain the magnetic properties even after it is removed from contact with the magnet. The practice of chanting Namu- Myoho-Renge-Kyo and studying and teaching Buddhism to others results in becoming one with Namu- Myoho-Renge-Kyo or, in other words, becoming enlightened. When you chant for the first time, the condition of Buddhahood may still be weak, just as the magnetic properties within the piece of steel are weak after just touching the magnet. Therefore, you may not be able to recognize the effect of Buddhahood.

However, the more time you spend chanting, the more consistently you chant every day, and the more determined you chant, the more you will see the various aspects of enlightenment emerging from your life. You'll begin to see yourself becoming happier, noticing the things in your environment more, noticing others around you, taking more pleasure in everything you do, enjoying your life more, inspiring others with wondrous new realizations, attracting people to you, changing the way you do things and the way you view the world, smiling more, laughing more, approaching new challenges with fresh determination, being more vital and full of energy, being more productive, feeling more confident, and increasing your inherent wisdom from within, and on and on. There are thousands more benefits that come from chanting, but we can't list them all here.

As you chant, these traits will become stronger and more noticeable the more you chant. This is what we call a strengthening of life condition.

Conditioned Genesis

I will include here for reference, a chart created for previous books that illustrates the relationship of the "Twelve linked chain of causation" also called the 12 Nidanna.

All the practices and science described in this book and defined by the core teachings of Buddhism are built around the primary concepts of "conditioned genesis", "impermanence", and "Ichinen Sanzen" (the three thousand realms experienced in a moment of life). The transcendental base of conditioned genesis, the 12 Nidanna (Pali) which, for the purposes of discussion we can treat as a "vertical" arrangement entering from the top at the first Nidanna, descending to the fourth Nidanna representing the "Potentiality" of the instantiation of a sentient "life", where we will combine with the "horizontal" 3 factors of birth, and then continue downward through the remaining Nidanna into the "Actuality" of the instantiation as birth, decay, death, and the return to the continuum.

Conditioned Genesis
Transcendental Base

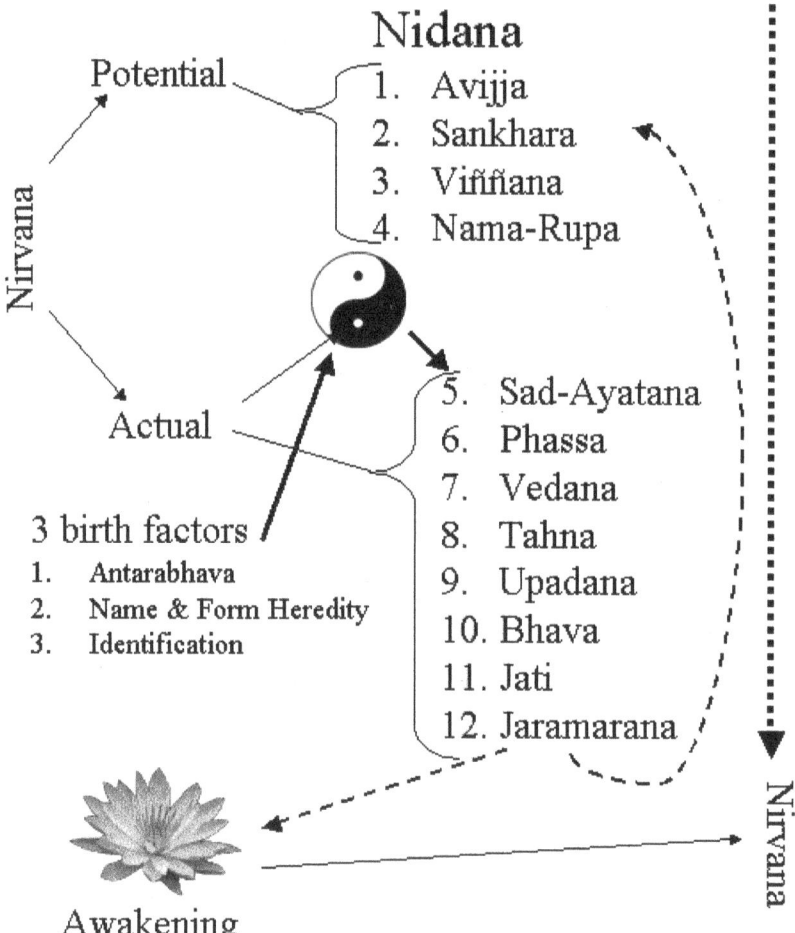

Nidana

Potential

1. Avijja
2. Sankhara
3. Viññana
4. Nama-Rupa

Nirvana

Actual

3 birth factors

1. Antarabhava
2. Name & Form Heredity
3. Identification

5. Sad-Ayatana
6. Phassa
7. Vedana
8. Tahna
9. Upadana
10. Bhava
11. Jati
12. Jaramarana

Nirvana

Awakening

As stated earlier in this text, the subtle consciousness is a state or non-state of "pure" awareness. The first Nidanna then is simply a subtle break from this subtlety as a thought, an idea, a gestation from a state of complete awareness. For the purposes of Quantum Life Buddhism method, I will be mixing Chinese, Sanskrit, Pali, and Japanese conceptual language into this English language to demonstrate the parallel and identical concepts and provide greater clarity of terms for a better understanding of the Buddha's teachings. We begin in the WUJI state of non-differentiated, ultimate reality. The thought or idea or gestation is the function of TAIJI, precipitated from the inherent tension of potentiality.

The twelve Nidanna:

The first three Nidanna can be understood as the subtle or Chinese YIN of differentiation or NOUMENA.

1) Avijja; Ignorance, unawareness. It is said here "Man is a God who is unaware that he is such". This state represents the initial stage for differentiation.

2) Sankhara; Predisposition. A state of volitional distinctions, this is the state where the parameters of the differentiation begin to form and identify themselves in conceptual ways. Also known as "Kamma-cetana", this is also where certain "imprinted" traits, or tendencies begin to "attach" and define the "fire" or passions, made of desire, aversions, fear and joy. This is also the initial stage of ICHINEN SANZEN as we collect Karmic Identity.

3) Viññana; Distinctive consciousness. The germ of all that will eventually appear as individuality and the "perception" of the Samsaric "I". From the fourth Nidanna we enter the polarized reality of YIN/YANG where the subtle Yin-Noumenal precipitates the Yang-phenomenal. This can also be related to the Samsaric germination stage of pregnancy. A successful pregnancy results from the conditions of the first four Nidanna of three entities, that of the female, the male and the new entity to be born. It takes three to make baby.

4) Nama-Rupa; Name and Form. This is the moment of the instantiation of all that is to "become" the Samsaric Identity. The creation of the differentiated phenomena using the 3 factors of birth as follows:

I. Antarabhava; The first three Nidanna, collectively the "Anta Rabhava", combine as the Samsaric entity from the preconditioned strain within all potential like the condensation of rain leading to waterfalls to become rivers and lakes.

II. Ichinen Sanzen; The Antarabhava joins the Nama-Rupa to insert itself as a particular group of Samsaric heredity (accumulated Karma). Truly the second stage of Ichinen Sanzen from which we form our unique experience of Samsara

III. Identification then follows infatuation (an affinity for an environment to flourish in which the support is conducive to the Samsaric heredity of this potential instantiation) by means of which the instantiation enters the womb and conception takes place.

At this point of the Nidanna and the descent into "birth", the 3 principles, Samkhya, of Karana, Linga, and Sthulsarira are in place. The Western equivalents are Nous, Psyche, and Soma or the Mens, Anima, and Corpus. This then is the genesis of the consciousness into an instantiation of "self-awareness" through the conditioned existence of Samsaric attachments to the world of "Name" and "Form", Yin/Yang, Self and Other.

This is the starting point for the personality or character that drives every aspect of our human manifestation including temperament, hair and eye color, and body type.

The 5th Nidanna can be related to our Samsaric concept of the "conception" stage of pregnancy.

> **5)** Sad-ayatana; Assumption of the six-fold base. The development of the sensory fields or strands appear at this point which, through "contact", the various sense impressions and various images of the instantiation will crave self-awareness. The six senses are:
>
> I. Touch
> II. Hearing
> III. Sight
> IV. Smell
> V. Taste
> VI. Thought

The 6th through the 9th Nidanna relate to our concept of fetal development ion the womb.

> **6)** Phassa; Contact or Touch. We now descend the vertical progression to the "Actuality" of the instantiation with the Phassa. This is the first contact with the physical world, the attachment to

the uterus wall, which then leads directly to Vedanä.

7) Vedanä; Feeling. This is the stage for affective "coloring" of the perceptions and sensations as a whole, the first physical instantiations of the attachments leading to the agitated "mania" of Dukkha.

8) Tahna; Thirst. Awakening of the sensory fields forming the desires for the continued experience of the sensations.

9) Upadana; To Embrace. A coming into possession in the sense of attachment or dependence. An affirmation of existence of "other" and thereby creating the sense of a "self" differentiated from "other" originating the sense of "becoming" in the Samsaric "reality".

10) Bhava; Becoming. Manifestation of the "will" to exist as the Samsaric "I".

11) Jati; BIRTH. The instantiation of predisposed consciousness into the phenomenal world of "Name" and "form", from the eternal "flow" or continuum strand of consciousness, which now adds a new, impermanent consciousness extant only in this phenomenal pretext in a state of Dukkha. This commences our lifetime in Samsara, our conditional "self"

12) Jaramarana; Decay, Old Age and Death. The instant of Jati is inseparable from Jaramarana. Becoming generates the become, grows old and dies. To this I paraphrase a quote from the great movie director Alfred Hitchcock who, when asked about his excitement at the beginning of filming a picture after so many months of preparation and planning he said, "For me the picture is already done and what remains is only a walking through of the finished product as I am already working on the next creation". This is very "deterministic" or seems to provide a strong foundation for the idea of "destiny". However, by practicing the Buddhist teachings to connect to our eternal essential "self" we can transcend and even modify all those attachments and associations made at the time of the 12 Nidanna that resulted in our current state. This is the amazing power of our human conscious state and our ability to "transcend" Samsara to the essential creative core of our "being". By doing so, we can reprogram our existence! In this mundane world and for all eternity.

The conditioned existence; thusly demonstrated to be conditioned, as such, by the Samsaric heredity; a Samsaric heredity, which will now be amended, added to, and which the pursuit of awakening, through the practice of the Ultimate teachings (Namu-Myohorengekyo) will purge and purify all 9 levels of consciousness to escape the pattern of Karma from our past. The "cycle" here is like a big wheel that only contacts the ground at a small point (Samsara) which when in contact with the path (practice), affects the turning of the wheel, and has the potential to escape from its continuous turning.

An interesting aside of this concept of conditioned existence is the Buddhist indifference to the arguments of "evolution" or "creationism" or whatever else. Creationism assumes a creator, which simply is not required and in fact negated by the Buddhist continuum. Evolution can fit without difficulty due to the Buddhist concept applicable to all sentient and insentient beings regardless of Samsaric heredity.

Related to the Nidanna the four truths of the Ariya stated at the start of this book as the Four Noble Truths, can be translated from Pali as:

1) **Dukkha**. State of suffering and agitation due to attachments to illusions of phenomenal world of insubstantiality.

2) **Tanha**. The origin of cravings, thirst for existence, for becoming, burning of the "will"

3) **Nirodha**. Destruction of the Samsaric state generated through the 12 Nidanna .

4) **Magga**. Method to realize the achievement of awakening and illumination. Remove the ignorance of the Avijja Nidanna by using the very "mind" that is presently deluded by "name" and "form" attachments.

And you have the basic premise of the practice of ascesis. This is the program for awakening and liberation achieved through the science of the mind; to use the meditations and teachings to understand, apprehend, control and finally to direct our minds.

For those of you who contend with the idea of abortion, it should be observed from the study of this chapter that the Buddhist reverence for life is tied to this idea that life has no beginning or end. We experience only a temporary form in Samsara as an instantiation with its own determinism. This renders the "start of life" argument moot, as it is an eternal entity with varied manifestations.

However, whether the Nidanna descent into Samsara results in an actual birth or death or anything in between is a function of all three participants, in that each of their Ichinen Sanzen or Karmic dispositions affects the process. So to the Buddhist the issue is simply a matter of respect for all life and to let the third entity in the pregnancy have every opportunity to manifest its karma. Life is precious, as it is our only opportunity to release ourselves from suffering through the awakening of our Buddha-nature.

Ten factors of life

Also, ten suchnesses.

Ten factors common to all life in any of the Ten Worlds. They are listed in the "Expedient Means" (second) chapter of the Lotus Sutra, which reads: "The true aspect of all phenomena can only be understood and shared between Buddhas. This reality consists of the appearance, nature, entity, power, influence, internal cause, relation, latent effect, manifest effect, and their consistency from beginning to end." This passage provides a theoretical basis for the principle of the replacement of the three vehicles with the one vehicle taught in the theoretical teaching (first half) of the Lotus Sutra. Since the ten factors are common to all life and phenomena, there can be no fundamental distinction between a Buddha and an ordinary person. On this basis, T'ien-t'ai (538-597) established the philosophical system of three thousand realms in a single moment of life, of which the principle of the ten factors is a component. While the Ten Worlds express differences among phenomena, the ten factors describe the pattern of existence common to all phenomena. For example, both the state of hell and the state of Buddhahood, different as they are, have the ten factors in common. Briefly, the ten factors are as follows:

1) Appearance: attributes of things discernible from the outside, such as color, form, shape, and behavior.

2) Nature: the inherent disposition or quality of a thing or being that cannot be discerned from the outside. T'ien-t'ai characterizes it as unchanging and irreplaceable. The nature of fire, for instance, is unchanging and cannot be replaced by that of water. He also refers to the "true nature," which he regards as the ultimate truth, or Buddha nature.

3) Entity: the essence of life that permeates and integrates appearance and nature. These first three factors describe the reality of life itself. The next six factors, from the fourth, power, through the ninth, manifest effect; explain the functions and workings of life.

4) Power: life's potential energy.

5) Influence: the action or movement produced when life's inherent power is activated.

6) Internal cause: the cause latent in life that produces an effect of the same quality as itself, i.e., good, evil, or neutral.

7) Relation: the relationship of indirect causes to the internal cause. Indirect causes are various conditions, both internal and external, that help the internal cause produce an effect.

8) Latent effect: the effect produced in life when an internal cause is activated through its relationship with various conditions.

9) Manifest effect: the tangible, perceivable result that emerges in time as an expression of a latent effect and therefore of an internal cause, again through its relationship with various conditions. Miao-lo (711-782) regarded the Buddhist law of causality described by the four factors from internal cause to manifest effect as the distinctive characteristic of the ten factors. It concerns the cause and effect for attaining Buddhahood.

10) Consistency from beginning to end: the unifying factor among the ten factors. It indicates that all of the other nine factors from the beginning (appearance) to the end (manifest effect) are consistently and harmoniously interrelated. All nine factors thus consistently and harmoniously express the same condition of existence at any given moment.

Three realms of existence

The realm of the five components or as stated by the scholar Vasubandhu as the Five Aggregates, the realm of living beings, and the realm of the environment. This concept originally appeared in *The Treatise on the Great Perfection of Wisdom,* and T'ien-t'ai (538-597) adopted it as a component of his doctrine of three thousand realms in a single moment of life. The concept of three realms of existence views life from three different standpoints and explains the existence of individual lives in the real world. The five aggregates (components), a living being as their temporary combination, and that being's environment all manifest the same one of the Ten Worlds at any given point in time.

(1) **The realm of the five Aggregates (components)**:

An analysis of the nature of a living entity in terms of how it responds to its surroundings. The five components are form, perception, conception, volition, and consciousness.

1. Form includes everything that constitutes the body and its sense organs, through which one perceives the outer world.

2. Perception means the function of receiving or apprehending external information through one's sense organs.

3. Conception indicates the function by which one grasps and forms some idea or concept about what has been perceived.

4. Volition means the will to initiate action following the creation of conceptions about what has been perceived.

5. Consciousness is the cognitive function of discernment that integrates the components of perception, conception, and volition. It distinguishes an object from all others, recognizes its characteristics, and exercises value judgments, such as distinguishing between right and wrong. From another viewpoint, while consciousness is regarded as the mind itself, the components of perception, conception, and volition are regarded as mental functions. Form corresponds to the physical aspect of life, and the other four components, to the spiritual aspect. The principle of the five components explains how life expresses each of the Ten Worlds differently. Someone in the world of hell, for example, will perceive, form a conception of, and react to the same object in a

completely different manner than someone in the world of bodhisattvas.

(2) **The realm of living beings**:

The individual living being, formed of a temporary union of the five components, who manifests or experiences any of the Ten Worlds. The realm of living beings refers to an individual as an integrated whole, but since no living being exists in perfect isolation; it is also taken to mean the collective body of individuals who interact with one another.

(3) **The realm of the environment**:

The place or land where living beings dwell and carry out life-activities. The state of the land is a reflection of the state of life of the people who live in it. A land manifests any of the Ten Worlds according to which of the Ten Worlds dominate in the lives of its inhabitants. The same land also manifests different worlds for different individuals. Therefore, Nichiren says, "There are not two lands, pure or impure in themselves. The difference lies solely in the good or evil of our minds". In making this statement, Nichiren was countering the popular view that there are separately existing impure lands and pure lands. In addition, the three realms themselves are not to be viewed separately, but as aspects of an integrated whole, which simultaneously manifests any of the Ten Worlds.

Notes:

Printed in May 2023
by Rotomail Italia S.p.A., Vignate (MI) - Italy